Patience

Patience

A GUIDE TO SHANTIDEVA'S SIXTH CHAPTER

Lama Zopa Rinpoche

Compiled and edited by Gordon McDougall

Wisdom

Wisdom Publications
199 Elm Street
Somerville, MA 02144 USA
wisdomexperience.org

Library of Congress Cataloging-in-Publication Data for the hardcover edition is as follows:
Names: Thubten Zopa, Rinpoche, 1945– author. | McDougall, Gordon, 1948–
    compiler, editor.
Title: Patience: a guide to Shantideva's sixth chapter / Lama Zopa Rinpoche;
    compiled and edited by Gordon McDougall.
Description: Somerville, MA: Wisdom Publications, 2020. | Includes
    bibliographical references and index.
Identifiers: LCCN 2020001721 | ISBN 9781614296416 (hardcover) |
    ISBN 9781614296423 (ebook)
Subjects: LCSH: Śāntideva, active 7th century. Bodhicaryāvatāra. Chapter 6. |
    Patience—Religious aspects—Buddhism. | Mahayana Buddhism—
    Doctrines.
Classification: LCC BQ3147 .T54 2020 | DDC 294.3/5—dc23
LC record available at https://lccn.loc.gov/2020001721

ISBN 978-1-61429-835-9   ebook ISBN 978-1-61429-642-3

26 25 24 23 22
5   4   3   2   1

Cover photo by Lenny Foster. Cover design by Marc Whitaker.
Interior design by Gopa & Ted2. Typeset by Tim Holtz.

Printed on acid-free paper that meets the guidelines for permanence and durability of
the Production Guidelines for Book Longevity of the Council on Library Resources.

Printed in the United States of America.

Please visit fscus.org.

CONTENTS

EDITOR'S PREFACE

WHEN I was compiling Lama Zopa Rinpoche's teachings for *The Six Perfections*, the chapter on patience presented a major problem: it became longer and longer. This was obviously Rinpoche's favorite perfection to teach on. (His name, Zopa, does mean "patience," after all.)

The chapter needed serious paring down so that it wouldn't overwhelm the other chapters, but the teachings Rinpoche has given on patience are not just vitally important but also wonderful. When we looked to see if having a separate book just on patience would work, we realized we could structure it around the sixth chapter of Shantideva's *A Guide to the Bodhisattva's Way of Life*.

Rinpoche had actively taught on many of the verses of that chapter in the early Kopan courses, but there were sections he had not specifically covered. However, when I searched for teachings related to those verses, I was pleased to find nearly perfect matches. If you find that in a few places the commentary does not exactly reflect the content of the verses, I apologize. Probably, somewhere in Lama Yeshe Wisdom Archive's vast store of transcripts from Rinpoche's teachings, there are perfect ones, but I was unable to find them. Fortunately, these are very few, and mostly it is as if Rinpoche and Shantideva are of one mind. It was a joy to discover, as I compiled the book, that here was a complete commentary on this crucial chapter of one of the most important books in Tibetan Buddhism that also encompassed the quintessence of Rinpoche's teachings.

This has been a delight to edit. Long my favorite Buddhist text, I have read *A Guide to the Bodhisattva's Way of Life* many times, but working through the sixth chapter in order to compile this book has meant exploring it in a depth that simple reading doesn't allow. My hope is that, because each small block of verses is the core of a teaching by Rinpoche, you too can have the taste of going deeper into this profound and very beautiful text.

We have chosen to use the translation by Luis Gómez, from his *Introduction to the Practice of the Bodhisattva* (Wisdom Publications, forthcoming). With the publisher's permission, we have changed his prose translation into verse, as that's how the text traditionally appears. Other texts quoted have been cited.

So many people have worked so hard to make this book a reality. Not just the team at Wisdom Publications, and specifically Laura Cunningham, who I worked closely with, but also all the staff and volunteers who work for Lama Yeshe Wisdom Archive, painstakingly recording, transcribing, and archiving all of Lama Zopa's courses. I want to thank them all for helping to spread Rinpoche's words—words that are absolutely vital in this very fractured world.

I apologize for any errors found in this book; they are 100 percent mine. May this book inspire people to turn away from anger and selfishness and develop patience and compassion. May whatever merits gained from the creation of this book be dedicated to peace in this world, to the long life, well-being, and fulfillment of the wishes of all our holy teachers, especially His Holiness the Dalai Lama and Lama Zopa Rinpoche, and to the flourishing of the Foundation for the Preservation of the Mahayana Tradition and of the Dharma throughout the world.

Gordon McDougall
Bath, UK

INTRODUCTION

THE THIRD PERFECTION

Patience is the third of the six perfections,[1] which are practices to ripen the mind of the bodhisattva:

1. Charity (*dana*)
2. Morality (*shila*)
3. Patience (*kshanti*)
4. Perseverance (*virya*)
5. Concentration (*dhyana*)
6. Wisdom (*prajna*)

The nature of patience is keeping the mind in virtue whenever we encounter disturbance and harm. We, of course, could endure these with a nonvirtuous mind as well, which is why the distinction is made. There are three types of patience:

- the patience of accepting suffering
- the patience of disregarding the harm done by others[2]
- the patience of having certainty in the Dharma

Besides learning to not harm those who try to harm us and having patience when we are faced with suffering, we must have certainty in the Dharma and persevere no matter what hardships may arise when we try to practice it. There will certainly be hardships, but we must never forsake the Dharma, no matter how difficult it becomes. Without this strong determination, there will be little progress, and we can easily become lazy and waste our precious human rebirth.

The sixth chapter of Shantideva's *Guide to the Bodhisattva's Way of Life* (*Bodhicharyavatara*), the chapter on patience, is an extraordinary teaching on what patience is and how to develop it. In this book, we will use his entire chapter to explore the perfection of patience.

I also recommend that you read the ninth chapter, the chapter on wisdom, which complements the understanding of the advantages of patience with how things are dependent arisings and empty of inherent existence. Patience and wisdom together are the best cure for the delusions that are causing us suffering now.

SHANTIDEVA

Shantideva was born in the eighth century CE in India, near Bodh-gaya, where the Buddha was enlightened.[3] He was highly intelligent. When he was six, he meditated on Manjushri,[4] the manifestation of all the buddhas' wisdom, and not only saw Manjushri but also had a realization of him. Manjushri himself gave the young Shantideva many teachings, passing down the lineage of the profound path—the wisdom teachings—to him.

Because Shantideva was a prince, he was obliged to become king when his father died, but the night before the enthronement he had a dream. Manjushri was sitting on the king's throne, and he said to Shantideva, "The one son, this is my seat and I am your guru, leading you to enlightenment. We can't both sit on the same seat." When he awoke from the dream, he realized that he could not accept the crown,[5] and so he escaped, going to Nalanda,[6] where the abbot ordained him, naming him Shantideva.

Nalanda was a vast and wonderful place, the greatest seat of Buddhist knowledge in the world. Thousands of scholars studied, debated, and meditated there, and great pandits wrote incomparable treatises and developed incredible tenets on logic, as well as studied the sciences, art, medicine, and so forth. I can imagine that Nalanda was a very busy and vibrant place, and yet, outwardly, Shantideva appeared to do absolutely nothing. While the other monks studied, debated, prayed, did prostrations, engaged in debates, and did all the jobs around the monastery that were needed, Shantideva appeared to do none of these. The other monks could see none of his inner qualities and they became quite contemptuous of him, calling him *bhusuku*, the "three recognitions," which means eating (*bhu*), sleeping (*su*), and making kaka and pipi (*ku*)—the only things they ever saw him do.

In fact, Shantideva was a hidden yogi (*kusali*) who already had great qualities. He studied very hard and had realizations and secretly composed two texts: *Condensed Advice: A Compendium of Trainings* and *The Compendium of Sutras*.[7]

The other monks thought Shantideva should be expelled, so they devised a trick to get him out. They invited him to recite a sutra teaching, thinking he would disgrace himself and then be forced to leave the monastery. They built a very high throne without any steps, convinced that Shantideva would run away when he saw it. However, when he arrived, in front of the whole monastery, he asked whether they wanted a text from Shakyamuni Buddha or something not given before. Of course, the monks wanted something new—to really embarrass him.

Suddenly he was there on the throne and nobody knew how he got there.[8] Then he started reciting the complete *Guide to the Bodhisattva's Way of Life* by memory, like water pouring from a clear spring. In one session, without break, chapter by chapter, he explained perfectly and succinctly each of the six perfections of the bodhisattva's actions. When he reached the ninth chapter, the chapter on wisdom, he suddenly flew above the throne, flying higher and higher until he appeared no bigger than a fly, then he disappeared altogether. And yet the monks could still hear him teaching perfectly, as if he were still on the throne.

Needless to say, the monks were completely shocked at this amazing event. They had no idea he was a hidden yogi, a great bodhisattva, and a holy person with such great attainment of high realizations. The teachings he gave them had a profound effect on them. Those with heresy toward Shantideva developed great devotion. This was why he did what he did. A hidden yogi usually never displays his power, but Shantideva could see that this was what the monks of Nalanda needed.

After that, he lived at Nalanda and was treated with great respect by the other monks. He also traveled, and there are many stories about him. For instance, in Magadha,[9] one of sixteen great kingdoms of ancient India, he became a servant to a group of five hundred people who held wrong beliefs. Once, because there was a terrible storm lasting many days, their food ran out. Shantideva, as their servant, went out to beg and returned with one bowl of rice. However, when he shared it among the five hundred, it satisfied them all. In that way he showed them that their beliefs were wrong, and they willingly accepted what he taught them. There are many other stories like this.

Shantideva was like us, but he worked on his mind until he became completely free from delusions. In that, he is a great inspiration. There have been many yogis who have done this. What makes him so special for us, however, is his book *A Guide to the Bodhisattva's Way of Life*. Not only does it lay out everything we need to do to become enlightened, but it does so in a language that is beautiful and simple. It is a book that has inspired countless people since it was written over thirteen hundred years ago. It tells us that we, too, can develop our mind to the levels of realizations that the great masters have attained—and it shows us how to do it.

1 : ANGER DESTROYS ALL PEACE AND VIRTUE

VERSES 1–11

THE DISADVANTAGES OF ANGER

Shantideva started the patience chapter of his *Guide to the Bodhisattva's Way of Life* by explaining the terrible destructiveness of anger. Anger is the opposite of patience, and so, in order to develop patience, we need to first see the disadvantages of anger and the advantages of patience. When we understand this, it becomes easy to decrease and eliminate the former and develop the latter.

Anger is a very powerful mind, an agitated mind that wishes harm to what it perceives as the enemy: the being who has interfered with its happiness in some way. It is a mental state, not a physical thing—it is colorless and shapeless—but it can very easily lead to physical actions. When we see two tiny insects on the ground at our feet attacking each other, that is due to anger.

The object of anger can be a sentient being or an inanimate object—it can even be an idea—but the nature of anger is harm, the wish to harm that being or thing. Therefore it is a violent, intense mind. Attachment is often described as like oil that seeps into cloth, because it is almost impossible to separate the attached mind from the object of attachment. In the same way, anger is described as like fire, because it burns every good quality completely.

This is a good analogy. Living with anger is like having a burning coal in the heart. Just as a tiny spark can set off a grass fire that can destroy a city, a spark of anger can lead to creating harm that brings retaliation and then counterretaliation. In this way it can destroy lives. Like a fire can rage through our house and kill our family and destroy all our beautiful possessions, anger can rage through our life and kill our relationships and destroy any pleasure we might have. It destroys our peace completely. It grows into hatred and torments us with thoughts of revenge and the strong wish to somehow harm our enemy. Anger can destroy everything, and therefore it is often referred to as the most destructive negative mind.

Anger is the complete opposite of patience. Patience cannot be in our mind when anger is present. Anger is the mind that wishes to harm the other being—that is its function—whereas bodhichitta, the altruistic intention to attain enlightenment, is the opposite. Bodhichitta only ever considers the well-being of others, and so wishing even the slightest harm makes bodhichitta impossible. Therefore, patience is vital to develop bodhichitta.

Anger Destroys All Virtue and Peace

1 [A moment of] ill will destroys all of these good deeds,
    as well as generosity and worship of the sugatas,
    even if one has practiced them
    for thousands of cosmic cycles.

2 There is no evil like hatred,
    no ascetic discipline like patience.
    Therefore, cultivate patience actively
    by all means possible.

3 As long as the barb of hatred is in your heart,
    your mind will find no rest,
    no joy or happiness,
    it will have no rest nor steadfastness.

Our most urgent goal at present is to avoid the lower realms[10] in our next rebirth and to receive another perfect human rebirth.[11] The causes for such a human rebirth are very specific: perfect morality and great generosity, combined with the fervent wish to be reborn as a human. When we are angry, it becomes incredibly difficult to maintain any sense of morality. We might know that harming others is negative and yet we are helpless not to. It is easy to see how anger, because it destroys our merit, also destroys our potential to attain another human rebirth.

Along with heresy—for example, believing existent things such as karma to be nonexistent—anger is considered the most damaging mind to have in that it destroys any undedicated merit. Shantideva said that any virtuous actions we have created over thousands of eons can be destroyed in one moment of anger. Like grain that is completely burned in a fire can never sprout into a plant, any positive merit we have that has been burned by anger or heresy can never ripen into a positive result. Therefore, because we should do everything possible to overcome our anger, we need to think deeply on its shortcomings.

Even the merit we have dedicated in the strongest way, which might not be completely destroyed, is damaged by anger, and it might be many, many more eons before it can ripen. For instance, say we were about to realize bodhichitta tomorrow, but today we get angry. That will delay our realization of bodhichitta for hundreds—even thousands—of eons.

It is like we have done a job and expect to be paid for it tomorrow, but because we have caused some problem, our employer refuses to pay us at once. Maybe they write in the contract that we can claim the money after a hundred years—or a thousand or a billion years! Or maybe the money is in our bank account but we can't withdraw it until our next rebirth.

The destructiveness of our anger depends on not only its strength and length but also the power of the object of our anger. We shouldn't get angry at anybody, but when we get angry at something powerful, such as our parents or bodhisattvas, the effects are much worse. Our parents are powerful for us because of our relationship with them. Because they gave us this precious human body and have raised us with such loving-kindness, when we harm them by becoming angry, the negative karma we create is very powerful. It is said to be so powerful that we can even experience the result in this life. But that does not mean the karma is then finished. Because karma is expandable, we will have to experience the results of that one instance of anger for many lifetimes to come.

More powerful than our parents are members of the sangha. Arhats are more powerful than sangha members without realizations; and bodhisattvas, because they have attained bodhichitta, are more powerful still. To be angry at these beings creates incredibly powerful negative karma. It is said that just to glare at a bodhisattva disrespectfully is heavier negative karma than gouging out the eyes of all the beings of the three realms.[12]

Similarly, the actions we take with regard to one buddha are much more powerful than with all the numberless bodhisattvas. The most powerful being of all is our guru—the person we have made a Dharma connection with—and so becoming angry at our guru is the heaviest negative karma of all. Pabongka Dechen Nyingpo[13] explained that to get angry at our guru for the snap of the finger (which is calculated as being 65 moments, and there are 360 moments in a second), we must stay in the inexhaustible hot hell—the hell with the most suffering—for that many eons.[14] So, the damage a moment of anger creates is tremendous and depends on the level of realization of the being we get angry at. And if this is so for one moment's anger, there is no need to mention all the anger and negative karma we have been amassing since beginningless time.

That is why I always emphasize the importance of dedicating our merit. In this way, even though a negative thought such as anger may damage what merit we have accumulated, it will not completely destroy it.

Although many texts talk about the consequences of becoming angry with great beings such as bodhisattvas, that does not mean it is acceptable to become angry with ordinary beings. In the sutras it says we should not even become angry with nonliving things, not even a piece of wood; therefore, naturally, we should never become angry with an animate object such as a human being or an animal.

Whether we follow a spiritual path or not, we all need to overcome our anger. Because everybody wants peaceful, harmonious relationships with others, there is really no choice—we must do our best to develop patience. Even somebody who has no belief in karma and reincarnation can see the result of not being patient with others.

With anger there can be no peace. There is no greater hindrance to our journey on the path to enlightenment than anger. Because of this, we must do everything we can to protect our mind from this greatest negativity. Whenever we have the slightest sense that anger is arising in our mind, we must do whatever we can to avert it. The moment before anger arises, we can be sitting comfortably and contently, enjoying a sense of peace and happiness, and then, suddenly, there is anger, and all that is shattered. All of a sudden there is great pain in our heart as the flame of anger flares up, destroying both that moment's peace and our future happiness.

The remedy for hatred and anger is patience. As Shantideva said, there is no discipline like patience. To overcome the pain and suffering of the angry mind and destroy the inevitable suffering results that anger brings, we *must* cultivate patience. We must be so careful to watch our mind and never allow anger to arise, as if we are walking along a narrow path on the edge of a high cliff that we could trip over at any moment if we let our guard slip.

As Shantideva said in the first chapter,

> Only through the inspiration of the awakened ones,
> occasionally arises in a human being, for one instant,
> a thought directed toward the good,
> as lightning flashes for only an instant in clouded
>   night skies.[15]

Virtue is very rare, like the lightning in the sky, whereas our mind is like the nighttime without the moon or the stars—completely dark. We can only very rarely generate a virtuous thought and then only for the briefest moment. If that is so, how can we then destroy that precious virtuous thought by becoming angry? Unless we constantly stay vigilant and apply the antidote of patience as soon as we see anger arising, all our merit will be completely lost. This is what Shantideva means when he says there is no discipline like patience.

With anger we are completely unable to experience any peace at all. The moment anger arises in our mind it becomes uptight and agitated, like a knife going into our heart, like flames consuming us. While we have anger, no matter how comfortable or large our bed might be—with fluffy pillows, warm blankets, clean sheets, and even no fleas!—we are unable to sleep at all; the whole night is spent tossing and turning with the anger we feel for the enemy who has caused us such harm. Our heart is blazing with anger. We go over again and again the harm we have been done, how that person put us down so unjustly when we were so blameless.

Right through the night we concentrate on all the terrible things they did to us, creating more and more negative karma for ourselves. We try to remember every single thing—they did this awful thing, they did that awful thing, they said this terrible thing in this place, they said that terrible thing in that place. On and on and on. We don't meditate on how they harmed us in order to generate compassion for them but in order to justify our anger and determine how we can harm them back, if not physically at least with words. We think about the most hateful words we can say to them and our mind rejoices at how much it will hurt them.

If we manage to get to sleep, because we went to bed with anger, we experience terrible dreams, tossed about by our violent mind. After dreaming of harming the other person or being harmed, we wake up unsettled and irritable, feeling we haven't slept at all.

At nighttime we go to bed with anger, in the morning we get up with anger. During all these hours we live our life with anger, accumulating so much more negative karma. Even in the daytime our body is uncomfortable, and we derive no pleasure from the things around us. The most luxurious house gives us no happiness; the most delicious food is tasteless for us while we have anger.

Say we have invited somebody to a restaurant and it has gone very badly because of the attitude of the other person. Maybe the food is incredibly special and expensive, where even the mushrooms cost sixty dollars a serving, but the person sitting next to us is in a very bad mood and insults us in some way. Maybe it is just a few words or the way they look at us, but our whole meal is ruined. Overwhelmed by anger at the other person, we eat too fast and hardly notice which dish we are eating. When we leave the restaurant, we can't even remember what the food tasted like; all we can think about is the horrible person we sat next to. Our mind is utterly focused on that, reciting an angry mantra in our mind—"How horrible they are, how awful, what a terrible person, what terrible things they said, how bad they are"—on and on like reciting *om mani padme hum*.

We can see how anger physically changes a person. Even if somebody may normally look very beautiful, when consumed with anger their face changes completely, even its shape. The expression becomes fierce and awful, the color changes, the eyes bulge—their whole demeanor becomes terrible. People are scared to even look at them. They might be dressed in expensive, fashionable clothes, with their hair beautifully cut and wearing loads of expensive jewelry, but nobody notices any of that; they see only their terrible, angry expression. When there is anger in the mind, there is no beauty at all.

Agitation that comes from a loss of peace is a shortcoming of anger that can be seen by the eye. When we are agitated with anger, our discomfort and misery are quite visible. Not only that, anger disturbs those around us, making them unhappy and angry. We lose our friends and cause our family to keep a distance. As long as there is anger and hatred in our heart, there cannot be even a second of happiness and peace.

We work so hard to gain a good education and get a well-paid job so we can be happy. But no matter how much education and wealth we have, we can never be happy while we are under the control of anger. Without a good heart, our education will bring us only pride and arrogance. I once read in one of Lama Yeshe's notebooks a note he had made from one of His Holiness the Dalai Lama's teachings: education shouldn't lead to pride; a truly educated person, a wise person, is humble.

While under the control of anger, we have not the slightest freedom. All that education and wealth is completely wasted. We harm ourselves and harm others. One person not practicing patience, controlled by anger, has the power to kill millions of people. They can destroy cities and even countries to get what their self-cherishing demands. As we saw in the last century, dictators under the power of hatred can endanger the whole world.

On the other hand, even one person practicing patience stops giving harm to other sentient beings. However many beings there are on this earth are saved from their harm and given peace. If there are two people practicing patience, all sentient beings on this earth are doubly saved from harm and given peace; if there are ten, then the peace and freedom from harm they receive is ten times. And it is the same for a hundred practicing patience, or a thousand, and so forth; the more people practicing patience, the greater peace and freedom from harm people receive.

So, whether all beings receive peace and freedom from harm from us depends on whether we practice patience or not. Now, you can see the great responsibility we all have—to refrain from harming other beings and to try to bring them peace and happiness instead.

With Anger, Others Turn against Us

4 The same who have been honored with his gifts and
        attentions,
    the same who he has sheltered under his own roof,
    wish to bring death to the landlord
    who is cursed with an angry character.

5 His own friends fear him; though he gives generously
    he receives no recognition or favors.
    In brief, there is nothing
    that can bring well-being to a wrathful man.

When we have anger, we alienate those around us. Also, we can even make enemies of our friends and make the kind people who benefit us go against us. People who work for us or need us in some way resent us and may even wish us harm.

This is very clear. People who rely on us will generally appreciate what we do for them. If they are part of our family or our employees, they will see that the things they have are due to our kindness and they will naturally want to show their appreciation. If, on the other hand, we are the head of a family or a large company and we are cruel and angry by disposition, the people who rely on us will not like us and may even turn on us.

Shantideva said others may even wish to kill us. This happens in revolutions when tyrants are overthrown, and there are many incidents where cruel masters have been murdered by servants. Even in normal businesses workers find ways of getting back at angry bosses. Because the employee is reliant on the employer for their wages does not mean they have to show love and respect. They can make the boss's life a misery if they want to.

Tired of being exploited, people start revolutions, throwing bombs and destroying cities in order to overthrow the country and get their own way. What has been built over many years with much hardship and money is destroyed in moments. This is what anger can do.

When anger arises, the mind is completely dark. Perhaps we know and have faith in the Dharma, talking about it often with our friends. But when we are overcome with anger, all that Dharma is forgotten. What we have learned about karma or refuge or any of the other subjects seems very far away. Our mind is consumed with anger, hatred, and the wish for revenge. There is great danger.

Our anger also incites anger in others. We might even cause our kind mother, who gave birth to us and raised us with such care, to become angry at us and wish to harm us. This might seem incredible, but we hear about it all the time, how families argue and fight with each other—parent striking child, child striking parent, smashing furniture, beating each other with bottles and things, even using knives and guns.

I heard a story about two robbers in Delhi who killed a rich family because of anger. It seems as though they were planning to kidnap the son and daughter to get money from the famous father who was, I think, an army officer. When the kidnappers had the children, however, they did terrible things to them; they killed the entire family, and they fled. Much later they were caught and sentenced to be hanged. Although they refused to speak, people said they were angry because they were so poor and the family was so rich.

If we are angry or impatient, even somebody who is now our friend may very well become our enemy in the future. When we want them to always do exactly what our selfish mind wants and dislike them when they don't, they can turn away from us, no longer wishing to be with us. Even if we try to win them back, through giving them presents and things, they won't take them, or they take them warily, not trusting us at all.

Having minds such as anger, irritability, intolerance, and impatience brought on by frustrated self-cherishing is a principal cause of the breakup of relationships, destroying peace and harmony between people. This is true between friends, family members, teachers and students, employers and employees. The practice of patience is needed everywhere at all times.

Shantideva summed up these shortcomings of anger by saying that nothing can bring us well-being if we are angry. Nobody lives happily with anger. We can easily see this. Because of anger there is absolutely no happiness now, in this life, and there can be no happiness in future lives. Although anger always looks to an external enemy to blame, we must see that it is only ever the inner enemy, our self-cherishing, that produces our anger. This is what destroys all our merit and creates such suffering for ourselves and others.

EXTINGUISHING THE FUEL OF ANGER

Anger Comes from Frustrated Desire

> 6 Whoever sees that anger is the one enemy
> that brings upon him these and other evils,
> and attacks it tenaciously,
> will be happy in this and the next life.

> 7 Discontent arises whenever our desire is contradicted
> or the undesirable occurs.
> When hatred receives its nourishment from discontent,
> it gathers strength and destroys me.

> 8–9 Therefore, I will destroy this enemy's nourishment,
> since the most unpleasant event will not perturb my
> satisfaction.
> In discontent I do not find the object of my desires,
> rather it makes me neglect meritorious action.[16]

Next, Shantideva turned to how to overcome anger. Unless we extinguish anger and its causes, frustration and dissatisfaction, we always create more anger and have to endure all the suffering it brings.

We naturally want to experience pleasant things and not experience unpleasant ones. When somebody helps us or our loved ones, we are happy; there is never any anger. I don't think any of us has ever thought, "I am furious with that person because they have made me very happy." Conversely, if somebody does something that harms us or our loved ones in any way, we become unhappy and easily become angry, wanting to retaliate in some way. That is why the frustrated, unhappy mind is seen as the fuel that feeds the body of anger, strengthening it into hatred.

We have been born in the desire realm with this body whose nature is suffering. While we are in samsara we must accept that there will be problems, such as sickness, aging, lack of money, relationship problems, and so forth. One of the principal sufferings of human existence is not getting what we want. We are drawn to a desirable object and suffer because of that desire, then suffer because we can't obtain that object. Or we suffer because, having attained it, we can't keep it, or we fear we will lose it. In that way, there is no satisfaction in feeling desire. There is a hole in our heart, one we try to fill with more and more objects of our desire, but it is fruitless.

That leads to unhappiness, dissatisfaction, and anger at not getting our way. The stronger our desire, the more frustrated we will feel, and the more anger and hatred will arise because of that. Whenever somebody interferes with what we want, we will be unable to not get angry at them. On examination, we can see that so many of the world's problems come from this frustrated desire.

We can even relate this to our health problems. Many illnesses, such as heart conditions and strokes, stem from stress and anxiety, all due to striving for a thing that is either unobtainable or not satisfying once we do get it.

Everybody wants happiness, peace, and freedom from problems, but very few see that following desire is *exactly* the wrong method to achieve this. We can never find satisfaction following desire, and frustration and anger will surely arise when our desires are frustrated.

There is nothing pleasant at all about anger. Irritation, agitation, impatience, sullenness, spite—all these sorts of negative emotions overwhelm us and refuse to give us one moment's peace, whereas when we have patience, we have genuine peace. There is no question of which is preferable.

It is not that anger and hatred are weak minds. With hatred our mind is incredibly focused on the object of our hatred and how to destroy it. We should turn that strength around to destroy the real enemy, focusing all our attention on what is really causing us such unhappiness. *There* is the target—our own anger. When an enemy comes to kill us and we can recognize that enemy, then we put all our effort into killing the enemy, aiming our gun or whatever we have with complete concentration. We destroy the enemy, shooting them or dropping bombs on them. Anger is that enemy, and we need to destroy it completely with patience.

Shantideva's advice is to overcome anger by destroying our dissatis-faction. At present we are like a little child playing in a sandpit, making things such as houses and cars with piles of sand, believing them to be real, and becoming attached to them. Then when somebody kicks over those piles, we get incredibly angry because our attachment has been disturbed.

If we could realize impermanence, we would no longer see those objects as sources of our true, permanent happiness, and so there would be no cause for anger to arise. Without attachment, there is content-ment; anger is impossible.

This is where the teaching on the eight worldly dharmas is vital; it is the fundamental Dharma we must learn. While we are bound up in the four desirable objects we crave—happiness, comfort, praise, and a good reputation—and the four undesirable objects we want to be free from—unhappiness, discomfort, criticism, and a bad reputation—we will always suffer, and we will always be prone to anger when our desires are frustrated. When we overcome the eight worldly dharmas, we destroy our dissatisfaction, the seed of our anger and hatred. We can only extinguish our anger by removing the dissatisfied mind.

This shows we must see below the surface situation, the external enemy that is harming us, and even below the anger that that situation produces, to the very core of our unhappiness, the dissatisfaction caused by our self-cherishing not getting its way. *Here* is the enemy. *This* is what needs to be destroyed.

We don't have to become angry when adverse situations occur. When we analyze the situation, we see there is no reason for becoming unhappy. Unless we can generate a happy mind, how can we renounce the unhappy one? We therefore need to reflect deeply on the benefits of taking on suffering voluntarily and so make a strong determination to not allow anger and frustration to arise, no matter what happens around us.

Perhaps we are doing a retreat. We are trying to meditate but out-side somebody is running around making a lot of noise. Or, between sessions, our friend insists on telling us the most fascinating gossip, destroying any concentration we might have had in the next session. All we want to do is meditate and there are so many reasons we are unable to. Of course, practicing Dharma is the most important thing, but if somebody stops us from practicing by disturbing us in some way, is that a reason to become angry? Being disturbed at not being allowed to be happy will not make us happy.

Anger is an unsubdued mind, and we should not let it arise at any time—to friend, enemy, or stranger, human or nonhuman. Even when somebody disturbs our retreat, we should not get angry. If such a situation happens, we should think, "If I get angry, what is the point of what I am doing here? All these offerings I'm making, all these prostrations I'm doing, all these practices are to subdue my mind and destroy my delusions, so it makes no sense to become angry while trying to do all this. What a childish, crazy thing to do. By doing this I will be destroying everything I have been working for." When we look at it, becoming angry with somebody for disturbing our meditations on compassion is absurd.

Our expectations disturb our mind, not the person outside. Blaming external circumstances only causes anger and destroys our own happiness. On the other hand, if we see there is nothing we can do about it, we can accept that and see there is no reason for anger. When agitation starts to occur in our mind, we can calm ourselves like this.

No matter what happens, we should not allow anger to be our response. It could be something huge, such as somebody stealing millions of dollars from our Dharma center; or something tiny, such as a slightly sarcastic remark about our appearance or a mosquito bite. Whatever it is, we should deal with it with patience, compassion, and loving-kindness, with the thought to only benefit others.

Even if somebody breaks into our house and carries off everything, we should think, "If I don't practice patience now, when will I practice it?" This kind person has given us the best chance to practice what we most need to practice. Unless we see how only somebody disturbing us can allow us to develop our patience, we will never be able to transform our mind. We might know the teachings very well and be well aware of the necessity of developing patience, we might be working hard for others, but because there is no opportunity to control our anger, there is no opportunity to develop our patience. Without that, realizations cannot come quickly.

We can know *A Guide to the Bodhisattva's Way of Life* by heart, reciting it to others and giving teachings on it. If we don't practice what Shantideva said, however, we might go for months without getting angry, thinking we are doing very well—but then, as soon as somebody disturbs us, immediately anger flares up. Then, we make ourselves miserable and destroy the merit we have accumulated with great hardship over countless past lives.

We let a day go by—a week, a month, a year—without practicing patience. Before we know it, our whole life has gone by without practicing patience. Then, suddenly, unexpectedly, death happens, and we have never developed patience, despite all the teachings we have studied and retreats we have done. At the time of death, it is too late to regret not having developed patience. There is nothing we can do then. Only now can we reflect on the necessity of having a patient mind and determine to develop our patience fully. This is what we must do.

Why Be Unhappy?

> 10 If there is a solution,
> what good is discontent?
> If there is no solution,
> what good is it anyway?

The next verse in Shantideva's text shows us there is no reason to become unhappy with any undesirable situation, either ones we can remedy or ones we cannot. This verse should be remembered at all times because it gives us the reason we should never be unhappy; it is so effective for the mind.

If there is a possibility to remedy the problem, we should attempt to do just that. Seeing we can fix it, what is the point of being unhappy? We are just causing difficulties for ourselves by clinging to unhappiness when the solution is right there in front of us. As soon as we start to resolve the situation, the reason for having an unhappy mind disappears.

On the other hand, perhaps the situation cannot be remedied. Even if that is so, what is the point of being unhappy? It is useless. In Buddhist philosophical texts, space is defined as that which is empty of resistance; that is its nature. Maybe we don't like this fact—that space should be empty of resistance—but there is absolutely nothing we can do about it, so how absurd is it to be angry about it? There is no benefit to wishing that it might be otherwise. No matter how much we want it to be different, it will never change.

Say we dream of living in a palace made of jewels, with a golden roof, surrounded by a beautiful park, with swimming pools and thousands of snow lions and elephants—maybe golden elephants! However, when we wake up, we have nothing like that, not even one hair of a snow lion or one atom of a golden elephant. We want those luxurious possessions we had in the dream, but it is impossible. It was just a dream. It is senseless to torture ourselves with the thought that although we want those things so badly, we can never have them. There is no way we can make it happen, and no amount of misery and anguish can do anything about it. Wanting those things only makes us utterly unhappy. We need to realize that this is an impossible wish, let go of it, and just carry on with things as they are.

When we think of our current adverse conditions as miserable, we make ourselves unhappy. The more we dwell on how unfair it is or how powerless we are to change things, the unhappier we make ourselves. Such thoughts are useless and destructive; it is much better to accept a situation that cannot at the moment be changed.

This advice becomes particularly important when something major happens in our life. If we go for a checkup and our doctor tells us we have cancer, how do we deal with it? Although there might be nothing we can do to change the situation, at least we can change our attitude about the situation. Rather than becoming totally depressed, we can see that here is an amazing opportunity to transform our mind. Because other people have no thought of the impermanence of life, they waste this incredibly precious life. We, on the other hand, are aware of how little time we have, and so we must make the most of every minute.

Instead of drowning in our own problems, we use our cancer to see how so many others are far worse off than we are, and from that we develop deep compassion. From our own situation we know how the thought of dying with cancer creates great terror, and so we have great sympathy for those in the same situation. When we encounter somebody with cancer, we want them to be free from that misery with all our heart. From that compassion comes the wish to benefit them in whatever way we can, and so we dedicate our life to alleviating the suffering of those with cancer.

I have seen this many times with people who have a particular disease such as cancer or AIDS. Somebody who doesn't have the same disease might feel sorry for the sick person, but they will not have the same degree of compassion and empathy. Many, of course, turn away, rejecting the person through fear of the disease. There is a psychological difference between somebody who shares the problem and somebody who doesn't.

Clinging to an unrealizable goal brings so many problems, so the solution is to stop the clinging. In such situations, where there is nothing we can do, it is good to practice rejoicing. Say our partner has left us for another person. Rather than be driven mad with depression and misery, we can feel that they did what was best for them and they are making themselves and their new partner happy. Although we cannot remedy the situation, by seeing it in this light, we use it to create positive karma that will result in happiness in the future.

Rather than feeling jealous of those who have what we cannot have, we can rejoice in their good fortune. When somebody has success at work or in the Dharma, or they have a wonderful house or luxurious possessions or plenty of friends, and we don't, we should simply rejoice for that person without a shred of jealousy. Jealousy interferes with us having success in the future, so it ensures that not only will we be miserable now, but we will continue to be so in the future as well.

When a friend criticizes us or leaves us, rather than feeling sorry for ourselves, we can think that this is exactly what we need. Our selfish mind caused this problem. In the past, we caused disharmony and now we are experiencing the consequences of that. Instead of suffering because of this, we can give the problem back to the selfish mind, destroying the one true enemy—our self-cherishing.

Until we have overcome the whole of samsara, we will have to face problems. We will continue to be harmed by other beings and by other events and circumstances, such as illness. As long as our mind is conditioned to identify such experiences as problems, more and more things will be problems to us. The smallest, most insignificant matter will cause great pain in our mind, and we will become upset very quickly. On the other hand, if we see undesirable conditions as beneficial, we will be happy. The more we see the benefits of facing problems positively, the happier we will be to experience them. Then problems will become enjoyable, as light and soft as cotton.

Accepting problems rather than rejecting them can make a big difference to our experience. It can not only help stop worry and fear but also turn our action into a Dharma action. Facing problems can help us develop renunciation, showing how the nature of all of samsara is only suffering, as well as allowing us the opportunity to act on behalf of all sentient beings rather than give in to suffering. And we can see the emptiness of the problem we are facing, and so use the problem as a means to develop wisdom in a way that is very difficult when we are overcome with attachment. In that way, problems become the best possible teaching.

This is the essence of the Mahayana thought-transformation practices.[17] Whenever we encounter a problem, rather than developing a negative mind and feeling aversion for the problem, we are happy that here is an opportunity to develop our mind. We can use problems to give us a stronger sense of refuge in the Three Rare Sublime Ones—the Buddha, Dharma, and Sangha—to eliminate our pride, to purify our negative karma, to practice virtue, and to train our mind in compassion and loving-kindness.

The Twenty-Four Types of Patience

11 No one wishes pain, humiliation,
    insult, and disgrace for himself
    or for those whom he loves,
    yet, he wishes them for his enemies.

In the next verse, Shantideva showed us that while we want happiness and to be free from any suffering at all, and we want the same for our loved ones, we don't feel this way about our enemies.

Just as we crave the eight worldly dharmas, we want the same for those we have affection for—our family and friends. We naturally want happiness, comfort, good reputation, and praise, and we don't want their opposites: unhappiness, discomfort, bad reputation, and blame. In the same way, we wish those we love to have the four desirable objects and avoid the four undesirable ones. For instance, just as we feel really unhappy if we are slandered, we feel the same if one of our family members or friends is slandered. It is as if we ourselves have been harmed.

For our enemies, however, it is exactly the opposite. We *don't* wish them to be happy or have praise from others, and so forth. We *do* want them to be unhappy, to be blamed by others, and so forth. We really hope that they will have not only a bad reputation but the worst possible one. Similarly, we rejoice when they lose their possessions or break up with their partner.

For ourselves, we need patience when we meet the four undesirable objects and when we have obstacles to obtaining the four desirable objects. Of the twenty-four types of patience often listed in the texts, these are the first eight types of patience, those in relation to ourselves. In our life we always have problems causing us misery and frustration, so we need patience to be happy when these things occur. With patience, our mind is not disturbed when one of the four undesirable objects occurs; there is no irritation or anger. When we must experience an unpleasant situation or fail to have the happiness we expected, we do it with patience. When we lose our possessions or cannot obtain what we need or want, we face it with patience. When somebody gives us a bad reputation or we are not recognized for some good work we have done, we accept it with patience. And when we are slandered and blame is falsely piled on our head rather than being praised, we bear it with patience. In the same way, when exactly the same thing happens to those we like or love, we need to practice patience. These are the second eight types of patience.

The third set of types of patience relates to enemies. In general, seeing an enemy unhappy makes us happy and vice versa—if they are happy, we naturally feel unhappy. This is how our mind works. Rather than being miserable and resenting that good things are happening to them, we should practice patience and rejoice for them. When we see our enemy happy and comfortable, when people are helping them, when they have a good reputation and people constantly praise their wonderful qualities, we should be happy.

Maybe we are having a lively conversation with our friends, totally involved in what they are saying, when suddenly one of them says something complimentary about our enemy. Immediately our mind becomes confused, unhappy. We sit there in silence with a dark face, feeling so jealous. Or we contradict our friends, telling them that person does not deserve that reputation, that they didn't do all those good things. Instead, at that time we need to practice patience.

Instead of experiencing hatred at the admiration others have for our enemy, we too should view it as a chance to also admire our enemy. Such a thought is pure Dharma, because it is exactly the opposite of what the self-cherishing mind wishes. Conversely, when our enemy must experience the four undesirable objects, rather than rejoicing, we need to practice patience and not let the spiteful mind arise.

To sum up, we need patience for everything. When we must experience suffering, we need patience. When we are treated badly, we need patience. When somebody insults us, we need patience. When somebody gives us a bad reputation, we need patience. When these things happen to our family and friends, we need patience. When good things happen to our enemy, we need patience. When bad things happen to our enemy, we need patience.

2 ⁝ LEARNING TO ACCEPT SUFFERING

VERSES 12–21

Because there will be hindrances as long as we cycle in samsara, we must learn to overcome any problems we face as we try to develop our mind. We should see how suffering is the very nature of whatever unsubdued mind arises, whether it is a pleasant, unpleasant, or neutral feeling. Whether it is anger, attachment, jealousy, or whatever, it has arisen because we have taken this container of contaminated aggregates,[18] this body and mind. Furthermore, understanding that this unsubdued mind is impermanent destroys the sense of permanence that gives it power, and understanding that it is dependent on causes and conditions undermines the false sense of reality it has.

Kadampa Geshe Potowa[19] said, "Death exists. That is why it happens." We can't experience something that does not exist, whereas because death exists, we must experience it. If we were to experience something nonexistent it would be a huge shock! Supposing we had renounced samsara and attained liberation, and then one day we became sick or died. That would be a shock because these are samsaric things and we have attained freedom from them. But while we are in samsara, under the influence of these contaminated aggregates, these things are bound to happen. We have created the cause and we are now experiencing the result.

Just as the beings of the animal realm bring suffering on themselves, we also do many actions while seeking happiness that create only suffering. The nature of the desirous mind is like that. It gets stuck on the object, and we have no freedom.

The nature of fire is burning; the nature of samsara is suffering. Just as it is better not to put our hand in the fire and get burned, it is better not to be in samsara and suffer. There is no use keeping our hand in the flame and hoping the fire will get cooler. That will never happen. And in the same way, there is no use wanting to stay in samsara and still not suffer. The whole point is to try to get out of samsara. Until we do, we must accept we are going to suffer, and when something unpleasant happens we should just think, "Of course this has happened. This is samsara! Whatever happens will be suffering in nature because I am living in samsara." So, there is no reason to worry.

In this way, we can meditate on the patience of voluntarily accepting suffering, seeing how suffering happens, how it is natural while we are in this unenlightened state. By thinking like this, the mind is naturally happy.

WE NEED THE RIGHT KIND OF PATIENCE

12 With great difficulty is one hardly ever able to reach
     happiness,
     but sorrow recurs effortlessly.
     But liberation only [occurs by] passing through sorrow.
     Therefore, keep your spirit steadfast!

13 The people of Karnata, who believe they are the children
     of Durga,
     vainly undergo the pains of fire and mutilation
     with the hope of liberation.
     How can I be so cowardly then?

We voluntarily take on suffering when we know how beneficial it is. Furthermore, when we see how unavoidable it is, we accept it more readily. The cause of happiness—virtue—happens only very occasionally, whereas the cause of suffering—nonvirtue—happens all the time. This is the nature of samsara. While we are in samsara we will encounter suffering, so it is worthwhile to practice patience, to accept suffering.

We should be aware of all the types of suffering—not just the suffering of suffering but also the suffering of change and pervasive compounding suffering—so we can identify them as they occur and not be surprised by them. Of the suffering of suffering we should understand the eight and the six types, such as the sufferings of birth, death, old age, sickness, and all problems that arise between birth and death.[20]

When we investigate our situation, we will see how rare it is to be completely happy, and how the suffering of suffering almost constantly occurs; our life is filled with either small or big problems all the time. Problems occur because we have this contaminated body and this deluded mind; they bubble up from this source like water bubbles on top of a stream come from the water itself.

We must recognize, too, how the suffering of change is also suffering. What we consider to be samsaric pleasures are also suffering by nature. Although they might give us some enjoyment for a short while, they do not last and the short-term pleasure we gain will definitely turn to some form of suffering. Our attachment to these pleasures means we are always chasing them and always being disappointed. These are also like the water bubbles on top of water, coming from the contaminated aggregates.

What we need to renounce above all is the third type of suffering: pervasive compounding suffering, which is the root of the other two. To do that, we must first understand that the nature of our entire existence in samsara is suffering because of these contaminated aggregates, and that until we overcome all our gross and subtle delusions we can never be free from this. That is why it is called "pervasive."

Seeing how pervasive suffering is, there is nothing to do but accept it and, if we can, use it to renounce the whole of samsara. Without suffering there can be no renunciation of suffering and so no liberation from suffering and no enlightenment. When suffering arises, there is no reason to be dismayed; it is just samsara. If we suddenly find we have a toothache or diarrhea or something, we shouldn't be shocked or think how unfair it is, how it shouldn't happen to us. It is just samsara. By considering the nature of samsara we can determine to not be overwhelmed by it, but to accept it and remain happy despite it. As Lama Tsongkhapa[21] said, we should see all of samsara as a pot of suffering and see that it is natural to experience all these problems. Why should we be shocked or dismayed when they happen?

Shantideva talked about the people of Karnata, present-day Karnataka, who showed a great deal of patience, but for what reason? Every year they underwent great austerities, but their motivation was deluded. They worshiped Parvati, Shiva's wife,[22] who was the one who stopped Shiva's austerities and caused his degeneration. In order to please her, her devotees fasted for three days, not eating at all, and burned and cut their own bodies.

In India today, people still hold festivals where they undergo terrible privations, cutting their bodies and enduring great hardships, competing to determine who can suffer the most, all for reputation. This is what Shantideva is referring to: bearing such suffering for no good reason, without one single benefit.

I remember seeing an escape artist once. It was quite frightening. He was completely bound with ropes and hung upside down, and then kerosene was poured over him and the rope above was set alight. He had until the fire reached his body to escape from his bonds, even though his hands were completely tied. There were thousands of people watching. He was twisting and turning, and ash from the burning material above him was falling onto his face. It must have really hurt. Somehow, something went wrong. He wasn't able to escape in time and his assistants had to quickly cut him down and extinguish the fire before he was badly burned, but I think he was still injured.

All that fear, suffering, and maybe even tragedy, all for some fame and money. This was his way of earning a living, and he must have trained for a long time to be able to do it. But even if he earned a million dollars from that one trick, it was utterly meaningless. He had incredible patience learning that trick and performing it, but it was the wrong kind of patience.

If people like that display patience for no good reason, why can't we have courage for the sake of liberation? This is a very powerful question from Shantideva. Of course it is worthwhile to bear whatever problems we encounter in order to practice the Dharma. For instance, we must endure hardships when we do a *nyungné*, the two-day Chenrezig (Avalokiteshvara) fasting retreat. Such a practice involves a lot of renunciation, having to withstand the difficulties of hunger and thirst in order to keep the precepts that go with the retreat. This is not meaningless suffering, however. We do this for all other sentient beings, to remove their suffering and lead them to the supreme happiness of enlightenment. It is greatly worthwhile to endure such suffering for such a powerful practice.

Caring for children requires a lot of patience, and it can very beneficial. But if it is done out of self-interest, then is it the wrong type of patience. If our motivation for caring for them is the worldly one of seeking happiness for ourselves in this life, then no matter how much we sacrifice our life for them, no matter how hard we work—not sleeping at night and working endlessly all day until we are utterly exhausted, bearing heat and cold, hunger and thirst—we are undergoing hardships only to create negative karma. All our actions become nonvirtuous because, first, we have acted through self-cherishing, and, second, the motivation is attachment to seeking the happiness of this life. All the trouble we have endured becomes work only for suffering.

The patience we must practice is virtuous patience. When everything we do for our children is only so they will be happy, that is selfless, positive patience. We can think of the kindness of those sentient beings, our children, who are the font of all our past, present, and future happiness. This attitude is Dharma, pure virtue, because it is unstained by the self-cherishing mind. The less self-cherishing there is, the purer the Dharma we practice. With this attitude, no matter what difficulties we experience, no matter what hardships we bear, this is the right patience—this is useful patience.

Raising children gives us the chance to practice all three types of patience: disregarding the harm done by others, voluntarily bearing suffering, and definitely thinking about the Dharma. Despite great problems, we never have the wish to retaliate; we voluntarily and happily

bear the problems, and, by going beyond worldly concern, we are thinking about the Dharma.

The correct practice of patience means we do not see our children as
objects to bring us happiness. We should not think with attachment "*my*
child this" and "*my* child that." It is not that we can't use the pronoun
my—that's not the problem—but we should not see the child as our
possession. Whether our mouth says it or not, if our mind holds the
thought that the child is there for us, for our enjoyment and happiness,
that is the self-cherishing mind in action. On the other hand, when we
feel that we are there to serve that other being, that is not self-cherishing
but cherishing others. This is true of all the beings we work for, not just
our children.

We all want happiness. Maybe we are tired, and we dream of having
a break, but without patience we can never truly have one; while the
mind is always disturbed, there is no chance of a rest. We can go to a
Western pure land such as Goa or Tahiti (I'm not talking about the
Western Pure Land of Amitabha!) where there are beautiful gardens and
mountains and wonderful beaches, but there is no rest for the mind; it is
always in turmoil. That is no real holiday. Resting the mind in patience
is the real break.

How to Accept Suffering

Everything Becomes Easier with Acquaintance

> 14 There is nothing that will remain difficult after practice,
>   therefore, if one first practices
>   with less severe afflictions,
>   even the greatest torments will become bearable.

> 15 Why is it that you ignore as useless
>   the sting of mosquitos, wasps, and gnats,
>   hunger and thirst, and other painful sensations,
>   or violent itch and similar miseries?

16 Cold, heat, rain, wind, travel,
    disease, imprisonment, beatings—
    do not become tender in the face of these,
    otherwise your torments will multiply.

Shantideva next explained that whatever we do will become easier the more we practice it. This is very important advice. Whether something is easy or difficult depends on how acquainted we are with it. It all depends on training. Say we have been living with bugs for a long time: fleas, bedbugs, and so forth. This becomes normal for us. Fleas in our clothes, lice in our hair—they don't bother us at all after a while. On the other hand, if we have never come across bugs before, if we are used to sleeping in a clean, soft bed and living a very luxurious lifestyle, to encounter bugs for the first time is a great shock. While there are fleas in our house we can't do anything. We want them killed or we want to buy a new house!

Training the mind in patience can be done for worldly reasons or for the Dharma. I mentioned the people in India who cut and burn their bodies and fast for many days—something we cannot do. They can do this because they have trained their minds to accept that suffering, mistakenly thinking it is worthwhile. It all depends on how the mind—the colorless, shapeless, immaterial mind—interprets things. Something we find impossible to do can be done by somebody else easily. For a person who seeks worldly pleasure, practicing the Dharma is extremely difficult because their mind sees it as difficult. On the other hand, they will persevere for what they dearly want—possessions, reputation, and so forth—no matter how difficult, willingly undergoing hardships and danger.

For a Dharma practitioner it is completely the opposite. All the hard work needed to gain possessions, reputation, and so forth seems utterly pointless, but they willingly accept suffering to obtain the happiness of future lives, liberation from samsara, and enlightenment. Whereas the smallest samsaric thing is unbearable, they are happy to do the most difficult Dharma work.

Shantideva said we should not be impatient with things such as heat, cold, insect bites, and so forth, because if we are, then we will become increasingly intolerant of them. Conversely, we need to slowly build up our acceptance of small sufferings so we can start to accept greater ones. Things that irritate us now, such as bad weather, can be the beginning of our training, learning to accept them for the sake of other sentient beings because we see the importance of developing patience on our road to enlightenment. Gradually, once we train our mind in these small sufferings, we can learn to become like the Buddha when he was a bodhisattva and give our body to a starving tiger.

Therefore it is greatly worthwhile to train the mind in patience in this way. If we live in a place that is full of snakes, mosquitoes, fleas, and bedbugs, it is like living in a palace full of jewels.

This was so of Buxa Duar, where I lived with Lama Yeshe for many years. A former concentration camp, where the British had imprisoned political prisoners such as Mahatma Gandhi and Prime Minister Jawaharlal Nehru, it was where the Indian government housed the Tibetan monks when they first fled from the Chinese invasion of Tibet.

It was a kind of mischievous place. Surrounded by huge, forested mountains where tigers and elephants lived, it was extremely hot in summer, and in the evenings it swarmed with mosquitoes. The beds were made from stripped bamboos and crawling with bedbugs that lived in the cracks of the bamboo. When the monks cleaned the beds every few weeks by hitting the beds with sticks, the bedbugs would fall to the floor in the thousands. Whenever we had to go outside to the toilet, we faced leeches and snakes. If it was raining and we opened an umbrella while squatting on the toilet, there would sometimes be a snake in the umbrella. Snakes nested between the roof and the walls and would sometimes fall through the cracks onto the beds of sleeping monks. In short, the place was full of creatures that bit and gave harm.

After we had been there for some time, however, we became used to these creatures, no longer thinking of them as threats. The bites and the itching, even the illnesses we got from them, weren't seen as any great suffering. I'm sure if somebody had gone there from a big city at that time—say, New York—they wouldn't have been able to stand even an hour. What Shantideva said is so true—we can get used to anything.

We should not be content with just having a small amount of patience. We must develop it to its ultimate. When even small irritations disturb us greatly, we will always find so many discomforts, so many harms. We sometimes see this with old people in care homes who find fault with everything. While for others there are no problems at all, for these people everything is wrong. The weather is either too hot or too cold, too rainy or too sunny; the caregivers fuss too much or ignore them; the food is terrible. This happens when the mind is too concerned with the happiness of the self, when there is strong self-cherishing.

When we are too wrapped up in our own selfish happiness, the suffering we experience when facing small harms will increase. That does not mean that the harm itself increases, but our ability to bear it diminishes and so we suffer more under the same conditions. The more we are used to only sleeping in a big, soft bed, the more unbearable a small, hard bed will seem. Rather than just accepting it, we complain over and over in our own mind, like a mantra: "How uncomfortable, how bad, how uncomfortable, how bad." As we visualize all the wonderful, comfortable, huge beds we could be sleeping in, this small, hard one becomes smaller and harder and more difficult to bear. If we could be a little patient and learn to bear it, the harm would stop increasing; if we are able to bear the uncomfortable bed for one night, we will be able to bear it the next night, finding it progressively easier to sleep. In this way, our ability to withstand discomfort slowly increases.

Bearing hardships with patience is especially important for somebody practicing the Dharma. We can't expect to do a retreat, for instance, without facing any problems. We might wish to do a retreat but decide we need to wait until the retreat place is better, because the floor or the roof needs to be fixed and *this* is not right and *that* is not right—so many things need to be fixed before we can do a perfect retreat! Perhaps the roof will be fixed and we can start next week, but next week there will be another problem, and so we delay. If we must wait until everything is perfect and we never have to endure any discomfort, the retreat will never get done.

This is just an example, but we can see that when we are too concerned with comfort and easily irritated by small harms, our concerns distract us from our Dharma practice. Even our daily practice becomes weaker because of all the frustrations in our mind, and it becomes shorter until we no longer do it.

Whether we are experiencing irritation with discomfort or anger at a perceived harm, we need to train our mind in patience, developing our ability to remain patient more and more. The more we train our mind, the easier it becomes. Training the mind involves watching the mind, like spying on a suspicious character we think might be a terrorist. By always paying attention to what arises in the mind, whenever there is danger because a nonvirtuous thought starts to arise, we immediately practice the remedy, such as meditating on impermanence.

We can plan to watch the mind for a certain time each day, determining to not allow even a moment of anger to arise during that time, then we can gradually increase that time. We can determine to study Shantideva's patience chapter or some thought-transformation texts that we find are very effective for the mind and use those as a method to meet and overcome any thoughts of frustration or anger. This is a practical method to train our mind in patience, doing whatever we can to overcome any angry thought that arises.

We will certainly see changes when we observe our mind over a long period of time. At the beginning, there is no way of averting anger once it starts to arise. No matter what good advice we receive, we either disagree with it or find it very difficult to follow.

Perhaps our teacher explains about developing patience by remembering the kindness of the enemy. We might agree in theory but decide that that only applies to people who give trivial harm, whereas *this particular* enemy is completely bad, completely wrong, and the teaching doesn't apply to us. The teacher must have been talking about some other enemy. Years later, we see how correct our teacher is and we can apply that training.

It becomes easier with practice. After a while we can start to see anger arising, like a beacon flashing or the landing lights of an airport coming on as the plane approaches, telling us this dangerous situation will happen. Even if in the early stages the anger has arisen before we have time to practice the remedy, we can still see the harm of allowing our life to be controlled by anger and determine to do what we can to diminish and then destroy it. Practicing in this way, the next time a situation happens that normally incurs our anger, the anger will be a little bit less. Over time we will see that whereas before, maybe a few years ago, we would have been angry for days, now, although anger still arises, it disappears very quickly. And then it just occurs for a moment or two, and finally it is not there at all.

The change will definitely happen, year by year, if we keep at it. Seeing how there is so much more peace now that the angry mind does not arise gives us the determination to practice patience even more. Now, having developed patience, even if we are scolded, beaten, or starved, our mind remains patient, happy, and joyful. We remember the kindness of others and rejoice in the opportunity to experience the suffering for their sake. No matter what we experience, nothing can disturb our mind.

We Can Learn to Accept More Suffering

17 Some attack with even greater valor
     at the sight of their own blood,
     others faint by the mere sight
     of the blood of others.

18 This is due respectively to the valor
     and cowardice of their spirits.
     Therefore, he who does not let himself be conquered
         by sorrow
     will vanquish all afflictions.

When they are wounded in a battle and see their own blood, some brave people become even fiercer in battle. They use the wound as an ornament, as a decoration, to show their bravery. Trained in bearing suffering, that person can not only withstand pain, even if badly wounded, but also use the pain to increase their determination. Somebody who is not trained, on the other hand, will not be able to bear it.

Shantideva's point is not that we should endure difficulties in order to be successful in worldly pursuits. People all over the world work incredibly hard but not to develop realizations. When I think of this, I remember the Nepalese villagers, up at two or three in the morning every day to climb the high mountains, looking for firewood in order to be back before sunrise to sell it in the towns or outside people's houses. They get up in the dark and the cold, singing loudly to cheat the mind, to get the tiny amount of money that the firewood brings, just enough for a little food for a day or two.

When I am in the comfort of my room in Lawudo Retreat Centre near Namche Bazaar, I am encouraged thinking of them, how they work so hard for next to nothing, bearing so much hunger, thirst, heat, and cold. I think how, although I have listened to many teachings and know well enough what I need to do to achieve liberation from suffering, I am still so lazy, finding it hard to bear any hardships at all, not even a fraction of what they have to bear every day. If they could bear even a little of the hardships they have to bear but for the Dharma, the result would be great happiness in the future.

Most Westerners are generally not up hours before dawn, sweating in the burning sun all day, working incredibly hard on little food and not finishing until well after dark, bearing heat and cold, their feet cracking and sore. Still, I am sure you will agree, many Westerners work incredibly hard in their own way. What we must make sure of, however, is that we bear hardships for the correct reasons. Bearing hardships to create the cause of a fortunate rebirth where we will enjoy the results of virtue and be able to practice the Dharma is the correct kind of patience.

With No More Anger There Are No More Enemies

19 Even in pain the wise man will not allow
   the serenity of his mind to be disturbed;
   for he is at war with the perturbations,
   and in the battlefield pain abounds.

20 Only those who defeat their adversaries
   by welcoming on their bare chests the enemy's blows
   are true conquering heroes,
   the rest are merely slayers of the dead.[23]

21 Sorrow has another advantage,
   and it is that the shock of pain can bring about
   the downfall of pride, compassion for beings in
      transmigration,
   fear of sin, and love for the Victorious Conqueror.

Whenever we receive harm, we should not let it disturb our mind. This is what wise people do. Practicing the correct patience results not only in our own happiness and well-being but also in the happiness and well-being of countless others, as we have seen. The many wars that were fought in the last century and are still being fought are due to greed, hatred, and intolerance, all stemming from ego. They have caused millions of people to die and millions more to be terribly harmed, tortured, or displaced from their homes. With tolerance, this could never happen. Even on a domestic level, patience is the vital element, bringing harmony and happiness to a couple, a family, and a community. When we practice patience and accept suffering voluntarily, we become an inspiration to others.

There is no end to the external enemies we must destroy while we harbor anger. Therefore we need to refocus our attention to destroy our anger and other destructive emotions. Arya bodhisattvas receive no harm at all from others because they have eliminated all delusion, the cause for receiving harm. The number of enemies we have, the amount of harm we receive, all depends on the strength of our anger.

When we are free from anger, we are free from enemies. Without anger we cannot find any external enemies. If we have the concept of an enemy, we see an enemy; if we don't have the concept of an enemy, we don't see an enemy, no matter how others treat us. The great yogi Naropa said that when we are sick, the concept is sick; when we are born, the concept is born; and even when we die, the concept is dying. Everything is a concept.

The enemy is the view of our negative thoughts, an interpretation, a label. It is not the view of all our minds. It is not the interpretation of our positive, pure minds. In the view of patience, this being is the kindest person, the most precious one, because they give us the unique opportunity to practice. What we need to do is change our way of thinking, not eliminate all external enemies. As Shantideva said in the fifth chapter of *A Guide to the Bodhisattva's Way of Life*,

> Where will you find enough leather
> to cover the whole earth?
> Merely by wearing a pair of leather shoes
> you will cover the earth.

> In the same way,
> since I cannot control external objects,
> I will control my own mind.
> What is there to gain by controlling the rest?[24]

Imagine if, before a world trip, we told our friends we were buying many millions of square miles of leather to cover the entire surface of the planet so we could travel without getting thorns in our feet. People would think we were crazy. The earth is vast, and our feet are tiny. Rather than covering the earth with leather, all we need to do to protect ourselves is buy some shoes.

In exactly the same way, by protecting our mind with patience and awareness, we don't have to protect ourselves from external thorns of our enemies' harm. Without anger there can be no harm, even if our enemy owned countless atomic bombs. While overcoming our anger might be hard, it is possible, whereas being free from all external enemies without destroying our anger is impossible.

Therefore it is vital we attack our real enemy, the self-cherishing mind that generates negative thoughts such as anger, rather than those we currently consider our enemies. In *A Guide to the Bodhisattva's Way of Life*, Shantideva showed us the real battle. Worldly people will see the victor in a battle as a hero and call them brave, but the one who actually qualifies for the title "hero," the one who is truly brave, is the one who fights with the inner enemy, defeating the self-cherishing mind and its army of disturbing thoughts. Those who are considered warriors by worldly people might kill other human beings in bloody battles, but they are only killing corpses. We are all "living corpses" because we are in these bodies for such a short time. So whether we are victor or vanquished is of little consequence—a battle is nothing more than a fight between two corpses.

But, more than just accepting suffering, Shantideva showed us how we can use our disenchantment with samsara to generate renunciation and develop compassion. In that way, suffering is extremely beneficial. We see we are trapped in a cycle of suffering and will stay trapped unless we can finally destroy our delusions and karma, and so we develop strong determination to break free from all delusions. We develop a strong aversion to samsara.

We see samsara is nothing but suffering. Moreover, when we see we are entirely the same as all other sentient beings in being trapped like this, we dispel any thoughts of pride or arrogance. Having more power, more education, a more beautiful body, or more wealth doesn't help us. We are no better than all those other sentient beings who have been our kind mothers. Understanding how they too are under the control of suffering, compassion naturally arises. Because of this disenchantment with samsara, our self-cherishing diminishes and we cherish others more. And through that, we can attain bodhichitta and enlightenment. *That* is the way suffering is beneficial.

3 ⁑ OVERCOMING THE WISH TO RETALIATE

VERSES 22–52

LOOKING AT THE SOURCE OF HARM

Because All Delusions Arise from Conditions, Anger Is Inappropriate

22 I do not feel anger toward bile and the other humors,
    though they are the cause of great pains to me.
    Why should I become angry at conscious beings,
    they too are moved to anger by conditions they are not
        aware of.

23 As physical pain arises
    without being sought,
    anger also arises by force,
    even when not desired.

24 A human being does not become angry
    by freely deciding, "I will become angry,"
    and anger itself does not come into existence
    by willing, "I will arise."

25 All the manifold transgressions and sins
    are due to the force of causes and conditions,
    they do not exist
    as independent acts or entities.

26 And the conjunction of conditions does not have the will
    to think,
  "I will bring about this effect,"
  and the product also does not have the will to think,
  "I will be produced."

To step on a thorn and blame the thorn is ridiculous. The thorn is
just an external condition, a catalyst for our suffering. The real cause
is that we did not see the thorn, due to our lack of awareness and
ignorance. All the sufferings of samsara have external conditions and
internal causes, but we compound the suffering by not being aware of
this and thus blaming and getting angry at the condition rather than
the cause. If the cause of suffering were purely external, then there
would be no way we could overcome it and so we would all have to
suffer all the time. There would be no cure for the sickness of samsara
at all.

Just as it is pointless to get angry with the inanimate catalysts of
suffering, it is pointless to get angry with somebody who harms us,
because they are totally without freedom. Is the person who wishes us
harm different from the delusion that caused that wish to arise? When
we examine this, it is easy to see they are not the same. When we wish
to retaliate, we should remember this: It seems as though that person
is bad and has the voluntary desire to give us harm, but they are being
controlled by their unsubdued mind. Because the conditions have come
together and the main cause is there, anger uncontrollably arises and
they are powerless not to harm us.

Just as the illness that causes us distress does not volitionally think, "I
will cause that person harm," so the anger that arises in the other person
does not volitionally think it wants to harm us. Both are just results that
have arisen out of causes and conditions.

For instance, if we get a headache while we are in a retreat, that
headache is caused by the arising of previous karma, brought on by
conditions. The headache doesn't have the intention, "Now I will disturb the meditation by generating great pain." Or if we have a bout of

diarrhea, it is not as if the diarrhea decided it wanted to manifest just to keep us on the toilet seat and away from our meditation. Similarly, it is incorrect to think that the enemy intended to harm us and is therefore wholly responsible.

Even the cause of anger, the dissatisfied mind, doesn't decide it will become anger. Because of the frustration of not getting what the person wants, the cause is perfected and anger arises, without intent from their side. The dissatisfied mind doesn't decide to arise. The anger that grows from that dissatisfaction doesn't decide to arise. And, in the same way, the person who is angry with us doesn't choose to be angry. These all come from causes and conditions due to the unsubdued mind, and they arise without choice.

As Shantideva said, all the mistakes and negativities arise dependent on conditions, without freedom. They do not govern themselves; they have no self-control.

All suffering comes from the unsubdued mind. The suffering of birth, sickness, aging, and death, and all the other kinds of problems arise from it. All negative karma is caused by it, including the ten non-virtuous actions.[25] With the unsubdued mind, we are not only forced to create negativity and harm others but also to suffer through sickness, problems, and being harmed by others.

To complain about a person getting angry with us is as foolish as complaining about water flowing down rather than up. If we see some-body shouting at a waterfall, demanding the water flow upward, or complaining because the earth is not the sky, we feel that person is not right in the head. We know these things are impossible, and yet we don't consider that it is also impossible for the person who is angry at us to stop being angry because they are under the control of their delusions. If we looked at the reality of the situation, we would see this. Furthermore, rather than being an object of our anger, the person would immediately become an object of our compassion.

There are various reasons why we get angry. The first reason is that *we have not removed the imprint*[26] *of anger*. Whereas some people get angry even when they are given presents, others with compassion and little self-concern will not get angry when harmed. This shows that the harmful action is only the condition; the main cause of anger is within the mind.

If we have not yet destroyed the seeds of anger within our mindstream, when the right conditions arise we are helpless not to get angry. Every time we become angry, we leave an imprint on our mindstream that will cause us to become angry in the future, thus perpetuating and increasing our anger. The more negative imprints of anger we leave, the more difficult our future life will be. There is little we can do to stop anger when all the conditions come together.

When we directly realize emptiness on the path of seeing,[27] we finally destroy the seeds of the disturbing-thought obscurations[28] and cease all gross delusions such as anger, making it impossible for any delusion to arise: anger, attachment, jealousy, and so forth.

The second reason anger arises is that *despite knowing the remedies, we do not apply them.* Unless we let go of clinging to this life, anger will easily arise whenever our desires are frustrated. Only by practicing patience can we change that.

Until we have destroyed the seeds of anger by realizing emptiness directly, we must constantly watch our mind, not allowing anger to manifest when we see it is about to and, instead, practicing patience. As we have seen, how we view a situation depends entirely on our mind. Viewed one way, the person wanting to harm us is an enemy and the action is a harmful one; viewed another way, they are a friend and their action is helpful. When we are watching TV, we have the choice to switch channels, to a violent movie or a gentle one. Similarly, just as our mind is the door to all suffering, it is also the door to all happiness—depending on how we use it.

Everything depends on how we interpret the world around us. Say somebody loves us, but because of our own delusions we interpret that person's concern for us as self-interest and decide they don't love us at all. When we label them as unloving, we then believe it, even though that is not at all how it is. The problem has come entirely from our own mind.

Conversely, say somebody else really hates us. How we react to this entirely depends on our own mind. When we don't respond to that person's hatred with compassion and patience, that real human quality is missing, and there is no happiness or peace in our life.

Some of my Colombian students once told me about how dangerous life was in Colombia, with random violence and kidnapping and people being killed there every week. A lot of this has to do with the drug trade. And in the United States, there are often random shootings. After the shooting in the high school in Colorado in 1999,[29] there was a big debate in the government and on television that went on for months about whether people should be free to have guns, but there wasn't one mention about people controlling the mind and having a good heart.

At another time, after a supposedly normal person killed several people, an American news anchor demanded to know how this could happen. But at the same time he said there was no answer to stopping this kind of killing. I'm sorry to say this but he was wrong: *there is a way*. If these killers had met the Dharma and listened to the Buddha's teachings, they would know there is a method to transform their minds so that such things wouldn't happen. If they could have purified the obscurations that caused them to kill, that negative thought would not have arisen and the violence would not have happened. People might be shocked at what I'm saying but this is the solution.

If we can control our anger, we are like a real hero who saves a whole city from destruction. Without controlling our anger, we lose an incredible chance at happiness. We simply cannot comprehend what we lose when we give in to anger. That loss is incalculable; it is so much worse than losing a million dollars, than losing a billion dollars. Perhaps we get angry at an enemy and make them give us a billion dollars. We are richer by a billion dollars, but we must face eons of the most terrible suffering in the lower realms because of that anger, without a cent, without a rag to cover us or a scrap of food.

THE ULTIMATE AND CONVENTIONAL REASONS WHY ANGER IS INAPPROPRIATE

The Ultimate Reason Why Anger Is Inappropriate

27 The primordial substance proposed by some,
    or the self conceived by others,
    indeed could not be born
    by deciding, "I will be."

28 For, as long as the primordial substance has not arisen, it
        exists not.
    Who would be there to want to come into existence then?
    Moreover, once it came into existence it would not
        be able
    to cease from its active involvement with the objects of
        the senses.

29 Indeed, if the self is eternal, unconscious,
    then, like the sky, it is evidently inactive.
    Even if it could come into contact with other conditions,
    what sort of activity could the unchanging have?

30 Anything that at the time of an effect being produced
    remains the same as it was before the effect was produced,
    what part of the act of production did it perform?
    In the relation between this thing and the effect,
        which one of the two is the actual locus of change?

Here, Shantideva brings a meditation on emptiness into the practice of patience. Due to our current way of thinking, this person's action has attacked our self-cherishing, and so we react. We label that person's action as harmful and their state of mind as anger. Then that person becomes an enemy to us.

The self being harmed and the person harming appear to us as existing from their own side, and that is the fundamental mistake we make, the ignorance that binds us to suffering. The self, the aggregates, and the other person do not exist at all in that way. If we could see this, there would be no reason whatsoever for becoming angry.

That is not to say nothing exists. I, action, object—everything that exists—exists by being merely labeled by the mind. Phenomena exist no other way except by being merely labeled by the mind. No phenomenon exists from its own side; no phenomenon has inherent existence. However, not having realized emptiness, we are unable to see the I and other phenomena in that way. What we see is according to ignorance—that they exist independently, from their own side.

The merely labeled I has to relate to the aggregates, otherwise how can we point out where the merely labeled I is? For example, if somebody hits *you*, it means somebody hits your aggregates. There is no way somebody can hit you without hitting your aggregates.

We have a sense of I, based on the five aggregates, but rather than understanding it to be a merely labeled I, which does exist, we hold the I to be truly existing. This comes from negative imprints left on the mental continuum from past ignorance. This is the same with any phenomenon. Due to the negative imprints left by past ignorance, immediately after apprehending an object, the mind projects the hallucination onto it; it decorates the inherently existent appearance.

That projection is not considered the root of samsara, however. It is the moment after that, when the mind, seeing the object as inherently existing, *believes* it to be so. According to the Prasangika Madhyamaka school, that is the crucial moment. Immediately after apprehending the I as inherently existing, we believe that to be so, and all our mistakes stem from that delusion.

Everything comes from the mind, and everything is merely labeled by the mind—that is the reality. But to our deluded view, everything appears to exist from out *there*. That part is the hallucination. This nonexistent I is what we need to clearly understand; we need to realize it does not exist at all. Realizing that lack of inherent existence is the emptiness that frees us from samsara.

For beginningless rebirths, we have held on to this real I as 100 percent truly existing. Suddenly we realize there is nothing there to hold on to. It is like waking up from a dream where we won a billion dollars in the lottery only to realize that the billion dollars doesn't exist. In the dream we believed so strongly that we had won a billion dollars, but when we wake up we find we are just as poor. That real I that we have trusted and believed in is not there; it doesn't exist, and it has never existed.

How could there be an I that exists from its own side? We cannot apprehend an I other than existing on the aggregates, so it must depend on the aggregates to exist. Because there are the aggregates, we can create the idea of an I, a sense of self, making up the label upon those aggregates. This is what it means to be "merely labeled" on the aggregates. Because there are the aggregates, and because the mind makes up the idea—or the label—of the I, it is merely imputed by the mind. That means the I is *totally* empty; it doesn't exist at all from its own side.

The truly existing I, the hallucination, the one that doesn't exist at all, is placed on top of the merely labeled I, decorating it, covering it, like the houses in India that are always covered in cow dung. This real I is the kaka that covers reality!

The I that does exist depends on the aggregates, and so it is a dependent arising. At the same time, it does not exist independently, so it is empty of inherent existence. Therefore dependent arising and emptiness are inseparable; they are one in essence and different in label.

It is very easy to read the word *emptiness* in a Dharma text or hear it in a teaching but still not make any connection to our daily life. We can meditate on emptiness every day, but as soon as we stop meditating, we might still see everything as truly existing. As long as things in our daily life and our meditations on emptiness are unrelated, with one separate from the other, then no matter how much pride we might have, no matter how much we believe we are meditating on emptiness, it is totally mistaken.

For instance, while we are walking along the road, we need to see how everything is empty. We are empty, the road is empty, the action of walking is empty. When we go shopping, we the shopper are empty, the seller is empty, what we are buying is empty, the money we are paying with is empty. Everything is like that.

If we can see this, whatever we experience becomes a meditation. If we practice mindfulness in this way, relating everything to emptiness from when we wake up until we go to bed, everything becomes a meditation on emptiness.

The supermarkets or department stores in the big cities have billions of objects in them. If we see all those objects with this sense of emptiness, the more objects there are, the more we meditate on emptiness, and therefore the more they are a remedy to samsara. On the other hand, for somebody not practicing this emptiness meditation, who sees all these phenomena as inherently existent, the more objects they see, the more ignorance they have. Holding on to all those objects as if they were true, as if they exist the way they appear, means the mind is continuously blocked, obscured, from being able to see emptiness.

That is why it is very important to understand what *emptiness* means. In Tibetan it is *tongpanyi*, which is much more precise than the English. The *nyi*, which means "only," tells us this is not nothingness but being empty of any form of inherent existence at all. To realize the truth of all phenomena, the emptiness that is *tongpanyi*, is to realize how everything is a dependent arising. This is not the gross dependent arising but the extremely subtle one, the one according to the view of the Prasangika school.

This relates to Shantideva's questions. If the I, like the primordial substance that some philosophies propose, were inherent and therefore, being unrelated to any causes and conditions, could never change, how could anything ever happen? If nothing arises dependent on other factors, then nothing could arise at all. Suffering could not change to happiness; samsara could not change to nirvana.

However, because everything is a dependent arising, everything is possible. Just as suffering, karma, delusions arise due to causes and

conditions, so too does the cessation of suffering. By ceasing the grosser
defilements, we can cease all sufferings and achieve liberation. Then, by
ceasing even the subtle defilements, we can achieve enlightenment. This
is all because everything is empty of inherent existence.

The Conventional Reason Anger Is Inappropriate

31   Thus, everything depends on something else,
　　　and that on which it depends is also dependent.
　　　Under these circumstances, among entities, which, like mag-
　　　　　ical creations,
　　　lack self-activity, what should be the object of our anger?

32   *An Objector Interjects:* Then, it is also absurd to
　　　　　practice self-control,
　　　for, who could restrain what?[30]
　　　The Author Replies: It is reasonable to practice
　　　　　self-control, because there is causality.
　　　We thus accept that there is an end to suffering.

33   Therefore, when one sees that a friend or a foe
　　　has done wrong, one must remain at peace,
　　　reflecting, "Such and such conditions
　　　are the cause for his actions."

34   But, if only by one's own wish
　　　one could attain the object of his desire
　　　there would be no sorrow among all
　　　　　living beings,
　　　for no one desires sorrow.

Ultimately, the enemy who gives harm and the harm itself are both
empty. Neither exists inherently in any way. Because we are unable
to see it like this, we should train to see things as like illusions, like

dreams—maybe like hallucinations that happen when we take LSD! Because everything is dependent on other factors and nothing governs itself, these illusion-like phenomena are nothing to get angry about. It is like in our dreams there might be an enemy, but when we awake we realize there is no enemy there, existing by its own nature.

The enemy is like a dream enemy, but that does not mean they are actually a dream, that is, nonexistent. When we are meditating on emptiness, we must be so skillful not to fall into nihilism. In his *Four Hundred Stanzas*, Aryadeva said that believing that nothing exists— including the I and karma—and hence falling into nihilism creates karma heavier than having killed a hundred million people.

If the emptiness of the I meant there were no I at all, either truly existing or merely labeled, then nothing would exist. No suffering would exist; no pleasure would exist. There would be no need to move the body, no need to breathe. Everything would be completely pointless. Everything we do is to attain happiness and stop suffering, but if there were no I at all, none of our actions would have any effect. With no I, why have expensive treatments in hospital to cure the I that doesn't exist?

Many mistakes arise when we mistakenly think that the I doesn't exist at all. We meditate to try to attain a peaceful, happy mind, but this I cannot receive any peace because it doesn't exist. There is no karma, no cause and no effect. There is no point to anything and no reason to refrain from creating negative actions.

To think that because there is no I, no enemy, no phenomenon, and therefore nothing matters, we deny karma. That is a completely dark mind; it is very dangerous. Emptiness is not nothingness; meditating on emptiness is not watching nothing, like sitting in a helicopter looking at blank sky.

Nothing exists ultimately, but because everything is a dependent arising, everything exists conventionally, existing in dependence on causes and conditions. The enemy, the anger they have, the harm they give us, all arise due to causes and conditions. The suffering we feel from that person's anger has arisen due to karma, the negative actions we have done in the past, therefore we should not become angry in return.

For instance, it might seem that being criticized is a cause of anger, but if it that were so, then anybody who ever received criticism would have to get angry. That is not so. Somebody could criticize a buddha or a bodhisattva and no anger would arise at all. Even many ordinary good-hearted people will not react to criticism and other harmful actions.

A higher bodhisattva, who has totally renounced the self and only cherishes others, has still to remove the subtle imprints to knowledge, but all the grosser disturbing-thought imprints have been destroyed, so it is impossible to become angry even if somebody tried to harm them. Anger is only a condition; it is not an inherent cause. And because the cause is our own delusion, there is no reason to be angry at the person who has harmed us.

DELUDED BEINGS HARM OTHERS WITHOUT CONTROL

Why Be Angry with the Stick?

35 As a result of their own thoughtlessness
    some human beings will torture themselves with thorns,
        hunger, and other tribulations,
    due to their anger, and their desire for women,
    or other things that are not theirs to have.

36 Others will kill themselves by hanging,
    or jumping from a cliff,
    by taking poison or eating excessively,
    and through demeritorious conduct.

37 If, enslaved by the perturbations
    they thus destroy their own selves, so dear to them,
    then how could they be expected to refrain from bringing
        down
    these same torments upon the bodies of others?

38 Maddened by the afflictions,
    they act for their own destruction,
    they inspire only pity,
    how could there arise any anger for them?

39 If harming others is intrinsically natural to the foolish,
    it makes no more sense to feel anger toward them
    than it would be to be angry with fire
    because it is in its nature to burn.

40 On the other hand, if this defect is accidental,
    and living beings are by nature kind,
    still it would be as absurd to feel anger toward them
    as it would be to be angry with air when it carries
        fetid smoke.

41 If one forgets the stick, which is the nearest cause
        of pain,
    and feels anger toward the one who moves the stick,
    then it would be better to hate hatred,
    since it is hatred that moves the one who brandishes the stick.

Why do so many famous people commit suicide? Actors, singers, extremely wealthy people, and even highly educated people commit suicide. This is because, despite their material comfort, they are full of afflictive emotions. This is due to a lack of Dharma understanding, a lack of methods to transform their mind. They put so much effort into gaining fame and wealth but never try to transform their mind; and they are unable to control their delusions, which causes anger, jealousy, desire, and all the other deluded minds to arise. Then when they are overwhelmed with dissatisfaction, the thought of suicide arises. With all that wealth, education, and fame, they think the only way out is to end their life. It is very sad.

This even happens to people who are Buddhists. They might rely on the Buddha, Dharma, and Sangha, but they don't integrate the teachings into their life. Then one day, when, for instance, their partner leaves, what happens? Their life becomes a disaster. It is like how, in India, a fruit stall will have a big mirror and bright lights above the fruit to make it look all big and beautiful. But then you look at the fruit and it is pretty bad. Like the fruit in the mirror, their Dharma is just a reflection; it is Dharma without a heart. When a disaster happens in their life, their problems overwhelm them, they cannot practice Dharma, and so they commit suicide.

Nobody wants to suffer, but because we are overwhelmed by our delusions, we can't help it. Because of anger, jealousy, and so forth, we have disharmony in our relationships, causing arguments and fighting. Always trying to get its way, our self-cherishing creates all kinds of problems. We might get what we want for a short while—some comfort, some reputation—but because these things were gained through negativity, we will certainly suffer.

Like a moth to a flame, people run toward suffering. When a moth flies into melted candle wax, it becomes completely trapped. Its body and wings are so fragile that it is almost impossible to free itself from the wax. It doesn't think that the flame will burn its body—otherwise, of course, it wouldn't jump in—and yet the more we try to stop it, the harder it tries to get into the flame. It doesn't plan this in order to suffer; it only has expectations of happiness, and it is unafraid and unaware the flame will cause it suffering. Wanting happiness, the result is completely the opposite; the moth gets burned and dies.

If, because of their delusions, people are incapable of not harming themselves, then of course they will be incapable of not harming others. Why should we feel they harm us by choice, driven as they are by their delusions?

When somebody harms themselves or others, we should have compassion, like a son or daughter with a crazy mother. Even if the mother becomes crazy, completely uncontrolled, possessed by spirits, the child, knowing how incredibly kind and precious she is, sees that she herself has no freedom, and so she becomes only an object of compassion.

In the same way, we should see how whoever harms us is completely overwhelmed by disturbing thoughts that force them to create negative actions that only result in problems, now and in the future. Knowing that, there is no reason why anger should arise and why we should harm them. Becoming angry is totally inappropriate.

There are many reasons why this is so. It seems as though we are blameless and the other person is entirely to blame, but as they are ruled by their delusions, they have no control. At present we see the person and their anger as one, but they are not their anger. When we see that they are different from their anger, and that it is a delusion that is forcing them to act the way they do, we see things completely differently. They are without freedom, entrapped by their anger in the way the Tibetans have no freedom under Chinese rule or a person possessed by spirits is without freedom.

The person who harms us only wants happiness, and they think their action will bring them some happiness, but that is just their delusions speaking. They don't understand that harming another person can only result in more suffering. Because of their negative actions, when they are reborn in the lower realms, there is no chance for them to create any positive actions at all, so their suffering becomes endless.

We blame the person who harms us but that is incorrect. As Shantideva said, we don't blame the stick a person uses to beat us, because we see the stick is just an instrument in their hands. It would be completely silly to get angry at the stick. In the same way, the person is an instrument under the control of their anger and delusions. They are like a horse completely under the control of its rider or like our kind mother overcome by spirits. We would never blame her for any harm she does but instead blame the spirits that control her. Since the person is not responsible, instead of placing the blame on them we should blame hatred itself. Then rather than thinking of ourselves—*our* happiness, *our* problem—we think of the other person's suffering instead, and there is no choice—unbearable compassion has to arise in our heart. We see the person as so pitiful, with so much suffering.

LOOKING AT OUR OWN FAULTS

"My Karma Persuaded Me"

42   I myself during my past lives brought similar torments
      upon other beings. Therefore it is only fitting
      that this same tribulation should fall upon me,
      who is the cause of injury to other living beings.

43   His sword and my body are the twofold cause of my pain.
      He bears the sword,
      I, the body,
      with which one should I feel angry?

44   In the shape of a body I adopted this open sore,
      sensitive to the slightest touch.
      If I myself, blinded by thirst, bring upon it further affliction,
      what should be the object of my anger?

45   I do not desire suffering,
      yet I foolishly seek the causes of suffering.
      Since sorrow comes from my own offenses,
      why should I become angry at anything else?

46   The sword-leaf forest, the birds of hell,
      they all arise from my own actions,
      and so does my present suffering;
      where should I direct my anger?

One of the most forceful ways to overcome our anger is to see that we are being harmed because we have harmed others in the past. According to our self-cherishing mind, it is perfectly acceptable to treat badly the person who harms us—they totally deserve it—but it is utterly unacceptable that we are treated badly in any way—we are totally blameless. When we understand karma, however, we can see that because karma is definite, there is no way that we can be harmed by that person without having created the cause by having harmed them in the past. This is just the ripening of some past karma; we have created the cause and we are experiencing the result.[31] When we accept that this is so, the situation does not become a problem.

A negative action we did in the past has created the imprint on our mindstream that causes that person to harm us now in a similar way. When that harm is returned to us, we should think, "My karma persuaded me and now I am receiving that harm back." When we see that we are the cause of all this, how can we possibly blame them?

We should remember this in our daily life, especially in circumstances where there is a danger that we will engage in some heavy negative karma. Whatever we do in retaliation—angry words, a physical attack, a court case, or whatever—perpetuates the cycle of karma and ensures we will be harmed in the future. And because karma is expandable, from that one negative action we will have to experience the result for hundreds of thousands of lifetimes.

The person who abused us or robbed us is not the cause of our suffering; the negative karmic imprints on our mindstream have brought this about. Whatever bad situation we are experiencing can always be taken back to a similar negative action we did in the past.

Dharmarakshita's *Wheel of Sharp Weapons* is an extended teaching on this idea. The full title is *The Wheel of Sharp Weapons Effectively Striking the Heart of the Foe*,[32] which refers to attacking the *correct* enemy. There are two sorts of enemy: the external, physical one and the internal, nonphysical one. We normally see the external enemy as the cause of the harm that we must experience, but this text clearly shows us that it is the internal, nonphysical enemy that is our foe and that we must work to destroy. That foe is our self-cherishing, and the external enemy's action harms that self-cherishing. Dharmarakshita shows us how we need to turn our weapon around and attack the correct enemy, not the external one that is in fact helping us destroy our delusions. When we develop a deep understanding of karma, we will have complete conviction about this.

Every experience we have, whether it is happiness or suffering, comes from our own karma, from our own previous motivation. Karma is behind everything. External factors seem to be the cause of our problems, but they are just conditions. We are cheated by somebody only because they were cheated by us in the past; we cheated them and now we are being paid back. The karma has circled back, and it is our turn. When we see how we ourselves have brought this about, we cannot possibly become angry with them.

When somebody harms us with the weapon of harsh words or when we are bitten by a mosquito, these are results of our previous karma, of having had ill will in the past. We must understand that the bite is the result of our own negative action and the insect itself is blameless. We caused it; the insect is just the instrument. In the same way, if we are robbed of a billion dollars, the robber is just the tool of our own negative karma.

While worldly people generally feel that anger is the correct response to harm, seeing it in this light we can see how utterly foolish it is. Therefore if we want to be really smart, instead of returning harm with harm, we return harm with patience and compassion, benefiting the harmer in response to the harm we have received. If we can break that cycle, we will be helped by that sentient being for hundreds of thousands of lifetimes, guaranteeing ourselves so much happiness for all those lifetimes. In that way, the person who stole our billion dollars will be the one who makes us achieve enlightenment.

We don't receive help now because we didn't offer help in the past; we are poor now because we weren't generous in the past. Until we turn our habitual attitudes around, our problems will continue. To have perfect surroundings, perfect conditions, and perfect friends, we need to create the causes. It all depends on having a good heart, and then happiness comes naturally.

Causing Them to Harm Us, We Cause Them to Suffer

47   **Moved by my own actions,**
    there arise those who cause me injury.

Because of this they shall go to the [hole of the] hells.
Is it not the case then, that it is I who do them harm?

48 Because of them, by patiently accepting their offenses,
many of my sins will vanish. On the other hand,
it is because of me that they will end up in the hells,
where they will suffer for a long time.

Shantideva pointed out that not only is the harm we receive from some-body caused by our own previous negative action but also that by harm-ing us they are creating negative karma and so must suffer for it in the future. That means that we are the cause of their suffering. And most probably, because of their action, in their next life they will fall into the "hole of the hells." In other words, we are responsible for sending them to the lower realms. Seeing this, how can we not feel compassion for them?

The "hole of the hells" suggests a huge hole with terrible fires laid underneath. Being reborn in the hot hells is like falling through that hole into the raging fire, one that is almost impossible to escape. Once in the lower realms, it is extremely difficult to create any positive karma at all and therefore almost impossible to be reborn as a human being with a perfect human rebirth.

We are responsible for this, but that is not how a normal person would think. Most people would probably see any suffering their harmer expe-rienced as deserved, completely unaware that they themselves had any part in it. In fact, it is completely the opposite.

This is something we must remember in our everyday life. Whenever we encounter a situation where we can get angry because of what some-body has done, we must see how we have caused that situation and that they are powerless not to harm us and, in consequence, will cause them-selves great suffering in the future. If we retaliate with anger, because karma is definite and expandable, we too will suffer greatly in the future.

When Shantideva showed us that we are not only responsible for our own suffering but also the suffering of our harmer, he skillfully showed us how compassion, not anger, is the only appropriate response.

Furthermore, by responding to harm with patience, we will develop the positive qualities of our mind, all the way to enlightenment, so they are the cause of all our happiness, whereas because of having harmed us, they are faced with nothing but suffering.

The Angry Mind Mistakes Help for Harm

49 It is I who bring harm to them;
    they are my benefactors.
    Why do I turn things around, and,
    with a violent heart, give rise to anger?

50 If I do not end up in the hells
    it will be due to the qualities of my own disposition.
    What is there for these enemies to gain
    if I guard myself from impatience?

51 If I were to respond to their offense in this way,
    they would not be protected,
    I would lose my conduct
    and these wretches would perish.

Our friends cannot help us cultivate patience, only our enemies can. In that way, they are our greatest benefactors, and yet we mistakenly see them as harming us and we wish to harm them back. This is entirely the wrong way to think. The Kadampa Geshe Chen Ngawa[33] said,

> Therefore we must cherish those who cause us harm more than those who bring us benefit. Why? Due to an enemy's infliction of harm, we cultivate forbearance and thus obtain immeasurable merit. Because of our enemy's harm, we step up our efforts and traverse higher and higher levels. We thus attain all higher attainments, so we must cherish those who inflict harm upon us.[34]

When there is no patience, when we allow anger to rule us, it continues from life to life, causing us to harm countless sentient beings. It is very frightening when you think about it. Having anger creates more unpleasant situations and more reasons to get angry. We create more and more harm for others. We can see this in people around us. In history, there are people who have been completely controlled by anger who have started wars and killed millions of people. Unless we learn to control our anger, we can become like them.

On the other hand, if we could return the harm they have done us with compassion and patience, instead of giving the victory to our own anger and becoming its slave, we would give ourselves freedom. We would then no longer view the other person as an enemy or the situation as bad. Therefore we must develop patience, and the only way to do that is by being patient with somebody who is trying to harm us. As we will see, our enemy is really so kind to us by allowing us this opportunity.

Geshe Chen Ngawa's Four Ways of Controlling Anger

Geshe Chen Ngawa explained how to control and overcome anger by training in patience using four methods:

- by understanding that we receive the arrows of harm only because we have created the target of nonvirtue
- by meditating on loving-kindness and compassion
- by recognizing that harm and patience are like teacher and disciple
- by destroying anger through realizing the absolute nature of things[35]

The first way of training in patience is to understand that *we receive the arrows of harm only because we have created the target of nonvirtue*. This point requires a good understanding of karma. It relates to Shantideva's point, which we have already looked at—that our karma persuaded us to receive suffering.

Any negative action we do is a target for the arrows of harm. Lying to somebody lays us open to be lied to in the future. Stealing from somebody means we can easily be stolen from. Even looking jealously at somebody creates a target that can be hit by the arrow of harm in the future. Our target can be hit in this lifetime or in some future lifetime, but it will be hit, and it will be nobody's fault but our own. Therefore we should not be angry at the person who harms us, who in fact is only a condition in the situation that has manifested due to our karma. It is our own karma that is the real cause, and if we need to blame something, it is that.

Because we have created the target, others can shoot their arrows of harm. If, on the other hand, there were no target, there would be nothing for the arrow to hit. By creating negative actions, we are leaving ourselves open to receive harm in the future when the right circumstances manifest. That is the law of cause and effect; that is karma. The problem is not with the harmers and their arrows but with the target of negativity we have set up for them to fire at. It is completely our responsibility, completely our fault, and not the fault of the harmer. Therefore there is no reason to get angry with other sentient beings.

When we get sick, when somebody treats us badly, when problems arise with our work or family, when our cherished possessions break or are lost—whatever occasion arises that causes us pain—we need to see this is the ripening of the karmic imprint caused by some previous negative action we have done. Whatever difficulty we experience in life comes right back to our own nonvirtuous conduct. If we had not created the karma, we could not have received the result. The antidote, therefore, is to not create nonvirtue. Then we will no longer be a target.

When we get angry at somebody, we create a huge target. I think this is very easy to see. We get angry because we have been harmed and immediately we wish to retaliate. When we in turn harm our harmer and they then want to harm us back, who then is responsible for us being a target of their harm?

The second way of training in patience is to *meditate on loving-kindness and compassion*. This is so logical. If we really understand the position of the person we are angry with, we will see how they are suffering, how their delusions caused them to act in the way they did, and so instead of anger arising at them for having blocked our self-centered happiness in some way, only loving-kindness and compassion will arise.

When an insane person unwittingly harms us, we don't retaliate because we can see that they are not in charge, that the situation has been caused by their disturbed mind. In the same way, we need to understand that when somebody harms us, they are not in control but are being controlled by their delusions. What they do is without freedom, as if they are possessed by a malicious spirit.

In fact, the person possessed by a spirit is more fortunate than this person who has harmed us. Somebody will only be controlled by a spirit for a limited time; it is not something that has been going on from beginningless lifetimes and will continue forever. Sooner or later that person will be free from the spirit and recover. The person controlled by delusions, however, has been controlled since beginningless rebirths and will continue to be controlled unless they can free themselves from them. So, the "sane" person possessed by delusions, harming themselves and others, is more trapped than the insane person possessed by a spirit.

The third way to develop patience is by *recognizing that harm and patience are like teacher and disciple.* Having been harmed, we have an incredible opportunity to learn from our harmer. When we realize their role in leading us to enlightenment, we should feel so happy to receive their abuse. We are their disciple receiving their most precious teaching. As Geshe Chen Ngawa said, we should feel happy and meditate on repaying the kindness of this kind guru, seeing ourselves as the disciple who receives patience from them, and seeing them as the virtuous teacher who delivers patience into our hands.

Practicing in this way is not a pretense. We don't just pretend our harmer is a precious guru even though we know they are not. It is not just a mental exercise on our part. They really are the person who teaches us patience and allows us to attain enlightenment, and therefore they really *are* our virtuous teacher. Therefore, just as we respect and pay homage to the buddhas, the bodhisattvas, and the holy gurus, we should respect and pay homage to the enemy.

The final point of Geshe Chen Ngawa's four ways is to *realize the absolute nature of things*, which is emptiness. Of course, this is the most effective way to destroy anger. When we are angry, there seems to be a very real I that is angry with a very real enemy, but when we explore this further, it seems a little strange. We can look for this real I that is angry, but no matter where we look, we cannot find it. It cannot be other than somewhere in the body and mind—the group of five aggregates—but we cannot find it anywhere there. The five aggregates are not the real I, one of them alone is not the real I, and it is not separate from them. We cannot even find the merely labeled I on these five aggregates.

Similarly, when we look for the real, independently existing enemy, we cannot find it anywhere. We make up the label "enemy" and the label "bad," and we see the situation as inherently bad. There is the appearance of *bad* in our mind and we believe it. This is the view of anger. This has all come from our own mind. The appearance of a person as *enemy* and a situation as *bad* is the appearance of anger. As soon as we practice patience, however, that appearance of the person as enemy disappears.

Geshe Chen Ngawa said that the way to think is that there is no object of harm, no action of harming, and no harmer; that all of these are completely empty. We see that those things that appeared to us as real, as truly existing, are hallucinations of our deluded, angry mind. They are projections of that deluded way of thinking, like somebody on LSD seeing their body being cut to pieces. When we can understand this, there is no reason for anger to arise at all. In the ninth chapter of *A Guide to the Bodhisattva's Way of Life*, Shantideva said,

> Thus, among empty phenomena
> what can be gained, or lost?
> Who will be honored
> or despised, by whom?
>
> Whence will come pleasure and sorrow?
> What is pleasure? What is thirst?

If one seeks for its intrinsic reality,
where will one find thirst?[36]

When we awaken from this hallucination of having an enemy, we see
that no enemy exists from their own side. In that case, what purpose
does anger serve? None at all.

4 : OVERCOMING SELF-CONCERN

VERSES 52–97

LIFE IS TOO SHORT TO BE ANGRY

Why Cling to What We Must Soon Leave?

52 No one can destroy the mind anywhere
and by any means whatsoever, for it is immaterial;
yet, by clinging to it
the body comes to suffer physical pain.

53 Humiliation, offensive words,
and disgrace—these bandits
cannot oppress the body.
What makes you angry then, oh my mind?

54 Is it that the dislike of others
will consume me
in this or another birth,
that I try to avoid it so much?

55 Is it that I try to avoid it
because it is an obstacle to the acquisition of my fortune?
My fortune will turn to nothing in this very life,
but evil will remain the same constantly.

56 It would be better to die today
than to carry for so long this life of falsehood;

for, even if I were to live for long,
the agony of death would be the same.

57 In dreams a man will enjoy a hundred years of pleasure,
only to awaken later;
another one enjoys only an instant
and then awakens.

58 Doesn't the joy of both end
in the same manner upon awakening?
It is the same at the time of dying,
whether you have lived long or not.

59 Even if you gain numberless acquisitions
and enjoy many pleasures for a long time,
[you] will leave with empty hands, naked,
as if everything had been suddenly stolen from [you].

When we feel hurt because we have been criticized, the words of the criticism don't have the power to hurt us; the pain comes from our attachment to praise. Perhaps somebody is simply explaining our mistakes to us, but we immediately label it a criticism and get angry. But even if we don't have the mistakes that they say we do, there is still no justification for anger.

Just as it hurts when we are not offered a piece of cake when somebody else is, when we are insulted there is no physical pain but there is mental pain. Abusive words are only words. They don't even have to be harshly shouted at us; they could be sweet words said in a soft voice, but if the intention behind them is to hurt us, they can cause great pain in our heart.

If we didn't think we needed the admiration of others, we would not be unhappy to receive criticism; whether others admired us or not, whether we had a good reputation or not, our mind wouldn't get disturbed. The more we crave a good reputation or praise, the more being criticized hurts. Our mind becomes depressed and aggressive.

When people suddenly lose their job, even if it is because of redundancy and not because they have performed poorly, they very often feel that they have failed in some way. They suffer from low self-esteem and think that people judge them as a failure. Feeling they have been unjustly given a bad reputation, they can have a nervous breakdown or even go completely crazy.

When somebody disturbs our comfort, we need to practice patience. When we don't get what we want or get what we don't want, we need to practice patience. And similarly, when our good reputation is destroyed by what somebody has said about us, we need to practice patience.

If somebody has stolen something from us, we might think we have a right to get angry, but we need to examine this. If we look at how important our possessions, our friends, and even our body are in our life, we can see how much we will suffer because of our attachment to them when we are about to die.

One day, for sure, death will happen. Life ends and there is death—it is as simple as that—and there is nothing we can do. No matter how much fear we have, no matter how much we regret not having practiced Dharma and developed a good heart, death happens. Whether we believe in reincarnation or not, we die. Whether we have prepared for death or not, we die.

Everything we have ever cherished in this life is left behind at the time of death. Whether it is one simple teapot or a mansion with thousands of cars and dozens of swimming pools, it is the same to us now. We can't even take one strand of hair or one grain of rice into the next life. The poorest beggar and the richest billionaire are exactly equal in what they can physically take to the next life—nothing. All the wealth and power in the world is pointless at death.

Perhaps after long years of education we now have a well-paid job and have achieved a good standard of living with mountains of possessions. When we die, what will happen to all those things? Could we leave them today without any regret? Because one day, the day of our death, that is what we will have to do.

We also must separate from our family and friends. We cannot take them with us when we die. Our partner and children we love and who love us dearly are helpless in the face of our death.

We separate from our body at death, and that separation causes great suffering because, in some ways, our body is our most beloved possession. The body can do nothing for us at all at death. We have worked so hard for it all our life and then it lets us down by dying. We have taken such care of this body, which is soon to be a corpse: feeding it, clothing it, washing it, giving it medicine, giving it treats such as chocolate and alcohol. We bought it the most comfortable house and the finest furniture we could afford, so it could enjoy the best. While in one way it is our greatest possession, in another we have actually been its slave all our life, spending almost all of our time cherishing it.

Attachment to these things makes our death very difficult. They have complicated our life, and they will make us miserable at death. And dying with attachment means that we will almost certainly take rebirth in one of the lower realms.

Practicing the Dharma is the only thing that can help us at the moment of death. In the seventh chapter, Shantideva said,

> How can you enjoy eating, sleeping,
> and sensual pleasures while you are being closely
> watched by Yama, the King of Death,
> and all your exits are closed?[37]

Without the thought of death in our mind, samsaric pleasures will always be there to lure us away from what is important. We might be able to obtain whatever we think will bring us comfort in our life, but there is no certainty we will be able to freely enjoy it.

And even if we were able, what is the point of living a thousand years and always being surrounded by great wealth and comfort if we're not leading a useful life? To live a long life without any illness or discomfort solely for ourselves is an empty life. All we are doing is living longer in order to create more negative karma and ensure more suffering in our future lives. Without a good heart, no matter how rich or powerful we might be, there is a great risk that, because of our self-cherishing, we will use our power to harm others. We are dangerous to ourselves and others. The shorter we live, the less damage we will do, so isn't it better we die soon? Nothing gives meaning to life without a good heart. When we have a good heart, however, then there is a powerful reason to live a long time.

We should constantly be aware of death. When we wake up, our first thought should be, "This may be the last time I wake up in a human body." When we get dressed, we should think, "This may be the last time I put on clothes. Somebody else may have to remove them from my corpse." When we put the kettle on to boil water for a cup of tea, we should think, "I may die before the water has boiled." In the same way, we see each action we do as being possibly our last.

We can also start each day with the thought of how amazing it is that we didn't die during the night. In *Friendly Letter*, Nagarjuna said,

> With all its many risks, this life endures
> no more than windblown bubbles in a stream.
> How marvelous to breathe in and out again,
> to fall asleep and then awake refreshed.[38]

This understanding of the impermanence of our life is a real tool we can use at any moment. It is something we need to experience, not just read about. When a mind of anger starts to arise, by remembering the imminence of death we can see how dangerous an angry mind is, and we easily avert it. Remembering death is a great protection.

Nobody escapes death; there is nowhere in the world or beyond the world we can go where we can escape death. Not even Disneyland! We can go to Disneyland to stay forever young and we will still age at the same rate and we will still die. We can build the deepest, thickest fallout shelter to protect ourselves from the nuclear bombs that could destroy us, as so many Americans did in the middle of the last century, but we cannot escape death. None of those Americans died from an atomic bomb, but most died, and those still alive will die one day. We can bury ourselves in the middle of a huge mountain made of diamonds, something so solid and indestructible, but that will not stop death. There is no sanctuary that will hide us from death.

A popular quote says,

> You cannot be sure which will come first,
> tomorrow or the next life.
> Therefore, do not put effort into tomorrow's plans
> but instead it is worthwhile to attend to the next life.

Perhaps we will still be alive tomorrow. Who knows? But we can be 100 percent certain that there is no certainty that we will be. *That* is certain. Without that certainty, will we have the strength to go against our habitual tendency to attachment and anger?

We need a strong understanding of impermanence and death to overcome anger, the most frightening mind. Having a mind of anger as we die ensures us of a lifetime of an unimaginable length in the terrible suffering of the hell realm. This is the worst possible thing that could happen to us and so we need to fear the mind of anger.

A Life Creating Nonvirtue Is Pointless

60   *An Objector Interjects:* **But, is it not true that as long as
        I am alive, by means of my fortune and possessions
        I will be able to cultivate the good and destroy sin?**
        The Author Replies: **Do you mean to say that in this way
            the good would not be lost and evil will not increase,
        when you get angry, moved by desire for gain?**

61   **If the one single purpose
        of my life is lost,**

then what good is a life
that brings only evil?

62   *An Objector Interjects:* No, what I mean to say is that I feel
          hatred toward one who denigrates me
      because his ill will leads many living beings to perdition.
      The Author Replies: Why are you not angry then in the
          same way
      with those who insult others?

63   You are patient with those who show little love to others,
      when their disfavor has been produced by others,
      but you are not patient with those who insult you,
      though this also has been produced by a third factor: the
          afflictions.

There is never any justification for anger. It might seem we have a right
to be angry with somebody who blocks us from doing beneficial work,
but that angry mind can cause only suffering. If we die with an angry
mind, the harm will be incalculable.

Elsewhere Shantideva asks why we want no harm or disrespect for
ourselves or friends but just the opposite for our enemies. Here he is
asking why we are not at all disturbed when we hear somebody else has
been hurt by unpleasant words, whereas when those same words are
directed toward us, we are hurt.

If our enemy is harmed in some way, through criticism or whatever, we should feel the same way as we would for ourselves or our
friends; we should have patience. And when the enemy is admired,
we should feel happy in the same way we would if we or our friends
were admired.

What our self-cherishing wants is for us to be happy and for our
enemy—the enemy of our self-cherishing—to be harmed. If we were to
hear our enemy had become very sick or even died, our self-cherishing
would rejoice. So, to feel happy when they are admired is the complete

opposite attitude to how our self-cherishing thinks. In that way, it becomes pure Dharma.

Feel No Anger toward Those Who Harm the Dharma

64 Equally absurd is my hatred toward those
    who harm or desecrate images and shrines,
    or disparage the true Dharma,
    for neither buddhas nor their disciples and teachings
        suffer injury.

65 Put an end to your anger toward those
    who harm your teachers, relatives, and loved ones, etc.,
    by understanding, as before, that their aggression
        is born
    from causes and conditions beyond their control.

People can criticize the buddhas or even kill them; they can destroy holy objects such as statues and stupas, but from the side of the buddhas there is no anger at all. How can there be? A buddha has completely destroyed all delusions and developed all positive qualities so there is not even the slightest stain of delusion on their mindstream. Because there is no cause of anger, anger can never arise. This is true of even the higher bodhisattvas, those who have realized emptiness.

In *The Jewel Lamp*, Khunu Lama Rinpoche[39] said,

> How could someone in whom the bodhichitta
> of the supreme vehicle exists ever turn
> toward the poison of self-cherishing, even for a moment?
> How could they give up the nectar of cherishing others?[40]

When we have bodhichitta, there is no way we could ever harbor ill will toward any other being, no matter what that being might do to us. This is the power of bodhichitta. Our mind only ever thinks of benefiting other living beings, instinctively, spontaneously, without being told to do it. Having destroyed our own self-cherishing, we no longer harm others, and because of that, we are protected from harm ourselves.

Shantideva finished the first chapter of *A Guide to the Bodhisattva's Way of Life* by saying,

> I bow before these bodies
> in which is born the jewel of the sublime thought.
> I take refuge in these mines of bliss,
> from which one receives happiness even when one
>   offends them.

Whether a buddha or bodhisattva receives help or harm from us, they will feel the same degree of compassion. If one person offers perfume or a massage to them and somebody else cuts their flesh with an axe, they have no discriminating thought at all; they don't see one as friend and one as enemy. Living in the perfection of patience, they can never become angry no matter what occurs. No matter how much harm somebody does, that person only becomes the object of compassion for the buddha or bodhisattva. Therefore it is entirely inappropriate for us to become angry at somebody who harms holy objects.

Abandoning the Fire of Anger

Both Harmer and Harmed Act through Ignorance

66 Whether it is due to a conscious or an unconscious cause,
   sorrow is inevitable for all embodied beings;
   it is found in all sentient beings.
   Therefore, accept it patiently.

67 Due to their delusion, some offend,
   others, equally deluded, become angry at the offense,

which of the two shall we consider free of guilt?
And who shall we declare guilty?

68 Why did you do what you did in the past,
so that now you find yourself tormented by others in this way?
All beings act under the influence of their past deeds,
who are you to change this?

When we feel we are being hurt by somebody and want to retaliate, that is just the view of one thought: our anger. If we check, we will see there is no "person who is hurting us" from their own side and there is no harm. When we don't label the person "harmer" or the action "harm," they do not exist. It is just the view of our mistaken mind.

There is no reason to blame the other person for our harm. They are just a condition, whereas the cause is our own delusions. Say we put our hand in a fire. Of course we will be hurt, but it is pointless to blame the fire for burning us. It is our action that is the cause, triggered by our delusions. If we heard of a friend who committed suicide by jumping off a bridge, would we blame the bridge? We must look beyond the condition and see the main reason. If we have been harmed and become angry, the cause is our deluded mind, and specifically our self-cherishing.

When we get sick, we don't blame the illness. We look for the cause in many places—the food we ate, the climate, being under stress, and so forth—but we don't look for the real cause, the inner cause. Place, climate, diet—these things are conditions, but we rarely ask the important question, "Why am I suffering?" Unless we seek the main cause of our suffering, we will always use a mistaken method to overcome it.

For instance, trees, rocks, and so forth don't have pain because they don't have mind. Fire is hot and ice is cold, but fire and ice don't feel the pain of heat or cold because they don't have mind. If that is so, why does our physical body feel pain? Why do external conditions such as heat, cold, illnesses, and so forth cause our body to experience suffering? It is because the experience is created by the mind.

Then there is this question: Why can't we have a mind that doesn't create suffering for the body? When we investigate in this way, we can see that there is something in the relationship between the body and the mind that brings about suffering. If the mind were not deluded, there would be no physical suffering. However, until we can free ourselves from our delusions, we will continue to be plagued by all kinds of suffering.

Why, then, do we worry about the harm we feel from the attack of an enemy, but we don't worry about the deluded mind that has caused this? The enemy has attacked us because they are controlled by their delusions; we are harmed because we are controlled by our delusions. Which is to blame, the enemy's delusions or our own delusions? Are the delusions of the enemy any more to blame than the delusions within our own mind that brought about this situation? When we consider it, we cannot say that one is guilty and one is innocent.

All the problems and suffering we experience are the fault of ignorance, and specifically the self-cherishing mind. It forces us to do all ten nonvirtuous actions again and again, to kill and steal and lie, all to satisfy its demands. Whenever we experience difficulties, there is only one source of all those problems and we should put all the blame on that one. That source is neither an external factor nor our positive thoughts—our good heart, our compassion, our loving-kindness, our wisdom. It is the ego, the self-cherishing mind.

Not Allowing Anger to Spread

69 Still, because I understand this,
    I will devote my efforts to good,
    so that all these beings
    will carry thoughts of mutual amity.

70 It is like a house on fire—
    if the flames start spreading to another house,
    one removes the straw
    or any other flammable items.

71 In the same way, one should abandon at once
    all those things that could fuel
    the fire of hatred in the mind—
    for fear that the very substance of merit might be burned.

When we are angry at somebody, that will cause them to be angry with us. We have all seen this. Therefore we should guard our mind well, and never allow anger to overwhelm us. Otherwise it will take over like a fire in a house spreads from room to room. In *Eight Verses on Mind Training*, Langri Tangpa said,

> During all my activities I will probe my mind,
> And as soon as affliction arises—
> Since it endangers myself and others—
> I will train myself to confront it directly and avert it.[41]

Unless we constantly watch our mind and avert any negative thought that begins to arise, our anger can become stronger and stronger, taking over our mind. Then, because of that, we make others angry. Even if they weren't angry before, they become angry when faced with our anger, creating the cause for future suffering for both ourselves and them. Furthermore, our anger becomes an obstacle to realizations. When we see anger arise, we must immediately and forcefully apply the antidote in order to stop it.

We cannot be completely free from anger until we have eliminated its source, the self-cherishing mind. This is the demon we need to destroy. We should think of holding on to the self-cherishing mind as like holding on to a burning branch, or like having a red-hot burning poker thrust right into our heart. We can't stand it for even a split second, let alone a minute, an hour, a year, or the countless eons we have lived with this demon. Actually, the feeling of needing to be free from our self-cherishing should be billions of times stronger than the wish to be free from a red-hot poker in our heart, which would surely be only a small discomfort compared with the suffering that self-cherishing has inflicted on us since beginningless time. As Shantideva said in the eighth chapter,

> If one does not abandon the self,
> one cannot abandon sorrow,
> as one cannot escape being burned
> if one does not avoid fire.[42]

It is utterly meaningless to cherish the self the way we do. Cherishing the I, we reach out for objects of desire, and so dissatisfaction and then anger are never far away. Therefore this fundamental ignorance must be understood and destroyed. We should watch carefully, and the moment self-cherishing arises in our mind, we should avert it with all our might, unable to stand it for even one second. In its place we should develop the thought that cherishes others, the great thought of bodhichitta. This is the thought that brings all happiness—both temporal and ultimate—to ourselves and to others.

Whenever we feel exhausted in the middle of a retreat or some other Dharma activity, we should remember that we have died numberless times in beginningless lifetimes for meaningless things, creating negative karma through trying to gain material possessions and so forth. We have died so many times in wars or while climbing mountains, trekking, sailing, or surfing for pleasure. But we have never died for the Dharma; we have never died working for sentient beings. If we were to die today by fasting and doing prostrations, by bearing hardships to practice the Dharma, it would be a very worthwhile way to die.

A Little Pain Now Rather Than Great Suffering Later

72   Wouldn't it be fortunate if a man condemned to death
were freed after only cutting his hand?
Would it not be equally fortunate if one were to suffer pain
in this life instead of ending up in hell?

73 If you are not able to withstand
    even the insignificant pain of today,
    why don't you destroy anger,
    which is after all the cause of suffering in hell.

74 Thus, because of my own anger
    I have suffered in the hells thousands of times,
    but I did not achieve anything
    for myself or others with this suffering.

75 My present pain is nothing comparable to the pains of hell,
    and it will produce great benefits.
    It is therefore reasonable that I rejoice in this suffering,
    which will free the whole world from its suffering.

As Shantideva said, it is better for a person to have a hand cut off than
to be killed. When we practice the Dharma there will be hardships, but
no matter how difficult it becomes, it is much better than having to face
the suffering that will be the result of our negative karma, the result
that will certainly happen if we don't practice the Dharma. No matter
how exhausted we feel or what problems arise in our practice, that is
much better than experiencing the results of all those negative karmas.

    We don't need to talk about the lower realms—even if we were to be
reborn as a human, we have to go through problems again and again:
feeling hunger, being unable to find a job, running out of money, experiencing disharmony in relationships, fighting, and other difficulties.
We take rebirth again and again and experience this kind of life again
and again, going through the same problems, without any opportunity
to practice the Dharma.

    Therefore knowing that any hardships we face while practicing the
Dharma are purifying so much negativity in our mindstream, why
shouldn't we happily bear them? Even if we get very sick, there is no
reason for unhappiness; it is like having a hand cut off rather than
being executed. This is the core of the thought-transformation practices.

Rather than feel aversion for any problems we face, we see them as a means to get rid of our negative karma and accumulate positive karma, and so they are a source of all our happiness. In short, we transform suffering into happiness.

In the past, we bore hardships for possessions, reputation, and so forth, and all it brought us was rebirth in the lower realms. Now we are accepting a much lesser suffering in order to be free from that great suffering.

If we do a practice such as *tonglen*, where in meditation we visualize taking the suffering of all sentient beings and giving them all our happiness, possessions, and positive qualities, when we experience hardship we can think that we have prayed to take on the suffering of others and now it is happening. Now, because this suffering—cancer, relationship problems, or whatever—is manifesting, our prayers are being actualized. We should rejoice in that. In that way, we collect limitless skies of merit.

Finding Joy in Others' Happiness

Overcoming Childish Self-Concern

76 If others find joy and happiness
     in praising a person who excels in virtue,
     why don't you also rejoice, O mind,
     in praising him?

77 This practice will bring you an intense delight
     which is blameless, the source of further happiness.
     The virtuous themselves do not object to it.
     It is the best way to attract others to the path.

78 If what you do not like about praising others
     is that only the other person is pleased by it,
     then you object to all rewards, even that of payment for
          services,

**in which case, you have also rejected the future reward of
your present effort.**

When we praise somebody, telling others about their good qualities,
we create merit and make them happy. We also make ourselves happy.

The most beneficial praise we can give, in terms of developing our
mind, is to praise somebody we consider an enemy. This is because the
enemy is somebody who opposes our self-cherishing, and so by praising
them we are going against the desires of our self-cherishing. When we
praise sentient beings, we are in effect remembering their kindness, and,
of course, our self-cherishing can never see the enemy as kind. Therefore
this is like offering them the victory and taking the loss upon ourselves,
which is a key thought-transformation practice. This is a great remedy to
pride and utterly against the wishes of the ego. To do this, we have to be
very brave, and we need to really see the kindness of the enemy, not just
superficially but deeply. We need to use all the thought-transformation
practices and explore how only somebody who opposes us can give us
realizations and allow us to attain bodhichitta and enlightenment.

In the eighth chapter, Shantideva said,

> All those who live in torment in this life,
> suffer only because of their desire for happiness.
> All those who live in happiness, are in such a condition
> because of their wish to make others happy.
>
> But why say more?
> Simply compare these two:
> the fool who seeks only his own welfare,
> and the sage who seeks only to benefit others.
>
> Whoever fails to replace his own pleasure
> with the suffering of others will not reach, of course,
> the station of the Awakened, but neither shall he know happiness
> even in this cycle of transmigration.

What is more, even if you leave aside future lives,
even in this life if the servant did not carry out his work
or if the lord did not pay him the salary that is due to him,
no visible results would be obtained.[43]

These verses are a kind of conclusion, like a very clear outline containing the whole of the bodhisattva's path. In them Shantideva showed us that everything positive—all temporal and ultimate happiness—comes from cherishing others, from wishing others to be happy, and everything negative comes from only wishing ourselves to be happy. Therefore, by being happy when we see our enemy happy, we are defeating the self-cherishing mind and working toward enlightenment.

Small-minded concern for the self must bring unhappiness. When we consider it, we can see that this I we cherish so much is just one person, whereas others are infinite. No matter how many problems this I has, or how much pleasure and comfort, such things just relate to one being. How can we ignore all the other beings—all the hell beings, the hungry ghosts, the animals, the other humans, and even the gods and demigods—who are suffering so much? Working only for our own very limited happiness in this life and ignoring all others is childish.

We forget that every small happiness we have ever experienced is due to all these kind beings. Day and night we work only for ourselves, only ever concerned for our own interests, turning our backs on the suffering of others. We don't see their problems. When we have a problem, it seems like nothing else matters. Living like this is a very sad life.

Others are suffering so much, and we have incredible potential to help them, but we are locked in our own selfish concerns. If this were not so, we could lead them to not just a better human rebirth but also liberation and enlightenment. By ignoring them, it is like we have a human form but don't have a human mind.

When we think of ourselves as the most important of all living beings—which is how we act most of the time—we are completely hallucinating. Everybody wants happiness and nobody wants any suffering, but we forget that the only way to have real happiness is by cherishing others. What Shantideva said is very true, that the childish work only for their own ends, whereas the buddhas and bodhisattvas work only for others. There is no comparison.

When we see a holy being such as His Holiness the Dalai Lama, we can feel how his whole nature is bodhichitta. Ours, on the other hand, is completely filled with selfish concern, where nothing matters but the interests of this I that rules us. The contrast between His Holiness's incredibly peaceful, happy presence and ours is stark.

Without changing our attitude there can be no happiness, even samsaric happiness. As Shantideva asked, if we were able to be happy by not helping others, then why pay our employees? It is easy to see how ridiculous that argument is. Even in worldly terms, the employee must work for the employer to get wages to have a degree of samsaric happiness, and the employer must pay the employee to get their product made. If one decides not to help the other in this way, neither can be happy.

Therefore we must see the disadvantages of cherishing ourselves and the advantages of cherishing others. As Shantideva said in the eighth chapter,

> Whatever calamities, pains,
> and fears there are in this world,
> they all are due to grasping at the self.
> What will I gain by grasping at it in this manner?[44]

All the suffering we have ever experienced and will ever experience comes from this demon of the self-cherishing mind. When we see this, we can answer that question. We will gain nothing by grasping at it. It is no use to us at all.

We Should Find Joy Seeing Another Praised

79 When your own virtues are being praised,
    you wish that others may rejoice in them with you.
    Yet, when the virtues of another are being praised
    you do not wish joy even for yourself.

80 If you have given rise to the thought of awakening,
    by wishing happiness for all sentient beings,
    how can you now become irritated
    when sentient beings obtain happiness on their own?

81 You claim that you seek for living beings the state of
        a buddha,
    which assures them of the veneration of the three world
        spheres.
    Then, how can you burn with envy
    on seeing that they receive insignificant honors?

82 The person who nourishes those that you are supposed to
        support
    is in fact giving only to you.
    Why do you resent and not enjoy the sustenance
    your family has received?

83 He who wants awakening for all sentient beings—
    what will he not want for them?
    How could the thought of awakening ever occur
    to one who resents the success of others?

There is no happiness at all that does not arise from bodhichitta. It is the source of all the happiness of the buddhas, the bodhisattvas, and all sentient beings. Every single pleasure we feel, from a cooling breeze to a delicious drink, comes from bodhichitta, because it is the result of our virtuous action, which is generated by following the teachings of the Buddha.

There is nothing that compares to bodhichitta. All the universes filled with wish-granting jewels cannot compare. If we have bodhichitta we have the most precious jewel that takes us all the way to enlightenment. Therefore anything that blocks us from this inestimable mind must be overcome.

We say the refuge and bodhichitta prayers, praying that all beings achieve the state of buddhahood, but then we hope for our enemies to be unhappy or we feel miserable when we see that they have some success. That makes no sense at all. To want happiness for our friends but not for our enemies is to destroy any chance we have to develop bodhichitta, bringing suffering to them and to us.

We should practice patience by not being unhappy when we hear our enemy has received something good or not rejoicing when we hear they are suffering in some way. We can go further than that, however. We can rejoice when our enemy receives good things such as presents, praise, a good reputation, and so forth. We can learn to see them as others do and admire them too.

Not Enjoying the Suffering of the Enemy

84 If someone else does not receive the offering
    you wanted for yourself, it remains in the donor's house.
    It will not be yours any way.
    What does it matter to you whether it is given or not?

85 Should the recipient hinder the transference of merit,
    the act of virtue in the faithful donor, and his own virtue?
    Should he not accept, though he receives?
    Tell me, what would not make you angry?

86 Not only do you fail to regret the evil
    you yourself have done,
    you want to compete with others
    who have done good.

87 If some calamity came upon your enemy,
    what in it would give you satisfaction?
    What has no cause for its occurrence
    will not occur merely because you desire it.

88 On the other hand, if you could succeed in causing him ill
       merely by desiring it,
    why should there be joy in you when there is suffering
       in him?
    Even if there is some gain for you in his unhappiness,
    the resulting loss will be much greater.

To be angry at somebody for receiving something when we don't is the
mind of a child. Perhaps you can remember this happening to you,
maybe at Christmas, when somebody, an aunt or someone, gave your
brothers and sisters lovely presents but didn't give you one (or maybe
they gave one that wasn't what you wanted). Suddenly she doesn't love
you, and you hate your siblings. You shout and rage and storm out of
the room, throwing yourself onto the bed and bursting into tears. Did
you ever act like that as a child?

As an adult, we should be beyond that. If somebody receives something and we don't, by getting angry we create strong negative karma
that will mean future suffering—and we still don't have anything.
We need to go beyond this childish mind and recognize that it is the
self-cherishing mind that has been hurt, and that by not responding to
its demands, we are able to gain freedom from it.

Feeling gratified when we see that somebody who has hurt us is suffering in some way is also a very low mind. Finding satisfaction in the
suffering of another will lead to suffering.

It is possible to turn our attitude around. Rather than wishing harm
on our enemy, we can wish them happiness. We can even actively help
them. For example, many years ago in Sydney, an FPMT student held
a party that annoyed his neighbor, who retaliated by scratching the side
of his new car. Not knowing what to do about this, he asked George
Farley, an old FPMT board member, who recommended giving the
neighbor a present. The student thought this strange but decided to do
it, giving the neighbor a box of golf balls because he remembered he
liked golf. When he presented them, the neighbor didn't say anything.
Later, however, the neighbor went over to his house and said how much

he appreciated the gift. In that way, both families were happy, rather than developing animosity for each other. By giving the victory to the other person, we gain and the other person gains.

Overcoming the Need for Praise and Fame

Praise and Fame Are Meaningless

89 For this apparent gain is the terrible fishing hook
of the fishermen, the afflictions.
From their hooks the guardians of hell
will purchase me to cook me in their pots.

90 Praise, fame, honors
will not give me
merit or long life,
strength, health, or bodily comforts.

91 But the latter are the goods desired
by a sage who knows what is of benefit.
One who seeks only temporary pleasures, on the other hand,
can dedicate himself to drinking, gambling, etc.

92 Some will even throw away their fortunes
and sacrifice their lives for the sake of fame.
But can one eat the syllables in words of praise?
Can one enjoy glory after death?

93 Like a child crying in pain
when his sand castle is destroyed,
my mind weeps
when it has lost praise and glory.

94 This praise is nothing more than a sound.
It has no thought of its own, therefore it cannot praise me.

The only cause for my joy
is the idea that someone else is happy for me.

95 What does it matter to me then,
whether someone else's rejoicing arises with respect to me
  or with respect to another?
This joy and happiness belong only to this person.
I do not share even a small part of it.

96 If happiness in me is due to them being happy,
then I should have the same happiness whenever another
  is happy.
Why is it then that when someone finds joy in the happiness
  of others
I find no happiness myself?

97 Therefore, if I rejoice merely at the thought of receiving
    praise,
there is no connection with this other person,
who is the cause of my happiness
and I am simply playing a childish game.

When a fisher puts a worm on a hook, it is not dead. Seeing the moving worm, the fish sees something to eat. It sees only pleasure; it cannot see all the suffering it will get by taking the worm, so it goes to the worm without hesitation. Then what happens? The hook gets caught in its mouth, and there is incredible pain and no way to escape. Then, before death, before the consciousness even leaves the body, its body is cut into pieces, causing it to experience unbelievable suffering.

This is similar to the mouse and the mousetrap. The mouse, seeing food in a mousetrap, goes in, thinking of the food as pleasure, as something worthwhile. Blinded by the desire for the food, it cannot see it will be caught and killed. It doesn't see the suffering involved in the pleasure. Samsaric pleasure is like this. Our attachment labels the object as good and we desire it, not understanding that suffering will result from our attachment.

We must see that all cyclic existence is suffering. What we think of as pleasure, what we crave, such as praise and reputation, is suffering. It will not bring us any happiness, and it will cause us terrible suffering in our next life.

We crave being praised and yet the praise is just a collection of words; it cannot bring us any physical advantage. We might seek pleasure in drinking alcohol or gambling, but these are at best transitory pleasurable sensations that cannot be sustained and will definitely end, turning into the suffering of pain. And, of course, we all know how a little drinking can lead to more and then to alcoholism. The habit of drinking becomes an addiction that destroys a person's whole life, consuming all their money and harming their family terribly. When they die, they usually have a horrible death and are reborn in the lower realms.

Everywhere we look we can see people looking for happiness in samsaric things, not understanding that such things can never bring happiness. They even risk their lives looking for happiness! Every year thousands of people climb Mount Everest, looking for happiness. It is very difficult getting to the top, but many make it even harder by choosing the most dangerous route.

People throw themselves out of airplanes. They have big packs on their backs, and they all get in a circle and hold one another's hands as they fall down to the ground. They trust their parachutes, but sometimes they don't work. People jump off mountains with only a bungee tied to them. I've even seen a man on TV shoot himself from a cannon. These people are all looking for happiness, and many for a good reputation, but they cannot succeed because their mind has not become the Dharma.

Until we can free ourselves from the mind that is attached to the eight worldly dharmas, we will always suffer disappointment and unhappiness. We will be like children making houses and cars in our sandpit and crying in despair when somebody kicks them over.

Samsaric pleasure is very deceiving. It looks like a very nice friend: one who flatters us, telling us how fantastic we are while always cheating us. This is like the description of the cannibals in one of the commentaries on the eight Mahayana precepts. We are in a land where there are many cannibals. From the beginning they tell us many nice things—how much they like us, how they would suffer so much if we ever left them. And we really believe them. But then after we have trusted them and decide to live with them, they eat us! This is just what samsaric pleasure does.

Gaining a good reputation requires so much effort and expense, and then when we have it, no matter how successful we are, there is always the worry that we might lose it all. There are many examples of people working ceaselessly and spending incredible amounts of money—millions of dollars—all for a good reputation. And yet they can never lose the pain in their hearts that they might lose that reputation.

Even though Elvis Presley was the most successful entertainer in the world, the year he was going to die, maybe while he was singing the last song, he was crying, his tears flowing out. He had achieved the best reputation in the world, had countless friends, and was immensely wealthy, but there was still such sadness and depression in his heart when he saw he was going to die and still hadn't achieved satisfaction.

Attachment to praise is dangerous but so too is aversion to blame. We get angry when somebody insults us, calling us a dumb animal, but if we called ourselves that, that would be different. And if they called our enemy a dumb animal that would be entirely different. Insulting words are just words. In themselves they have no power to hurt. It is illogical to get angry when they are directed at us but not at somebody else. If we hear a tape recording saying we are a terrible person, it does no good at all to smash the tape recorder to pieces.

We may think we have a right to get angry with the person who recorded it, rather than with the tape recorder, but again we should investigate that. The person is like the recorder; their body that produced the words is not to blame, and neither is their mind, which is as controlled by their delusions as the tape recorder is controlled by the one who recorded the message. To become angry at them is a useless thing to do, and only makes matters worse.

5 : THE KINDNESS OF THE ENEMY

VERSES 98–111

ONLY WITH AN ENEMY CAN WE PRACTICE PATIENCE

Our Enemy Protects Us from the Lower Realms

98 Praise and honor destroy my serenity
and the shock of transmigration.
They generate jealousy toward persons of virtue,
and resentment of their success.

99 Therefore, those who rise against me
to destroy my reputation—
are they not dedicated to keeping me
from falling into the evil destinies?

100 Wealth and honor are chains
for a person who, like myself, seeks liberation.
How could I feel any hatred
for those who release me from these chains?

101 Since I am rushing toward certain suffering,
how could I feel any hatred toward
those who stand in my way, like a bolted door,
as if the Buddha had placed them there?

The traditional way for Tibetans and Sherpas to make the soles of
shoes was to soften the leather using butter. Because of the stiffness
of untreated leather, it could only be cut or sewn with great difficulty.

Therefore it was soaked in the butter left over from butter lamps and kneaded while drying in the sun, and polished to make it soft and malleable but still extremely strong. The kneading was a bit like kneading dough, working with the feet, pulling and pushing, until it became softer. When I was very small, my first teacher who taught me the alphabet would sometimes do this while he gave me a lesson or I was reciting a text. It takes a lot of physical energy.

With the butter, the sun, and the kneading, the leather becomes workable; without them the leather would be so stiff it would be useless. Similarly, our "untreated" mind—when we are not living in patience—is stiff and useless. We need patience, and we need other sentient beings to allow us to develop that patience. The harm that somebody tries to do us, testing our patience, is like the stiff leather of our pride being kneaded. By helping us destroy our delusions like that, they are saving us from the lower realms.

In the thought-transformation text *Eight Verses on Mind Training*, Langri Tangpa said,

> Even if one whom I have helped,
> Or in whom I have placed great hope,
> Gravely mistreats me in hurtful ways,
> I will train myself to view him as my sublime teacher.[45]

When Atisha was in Tibet, he had a servant, Atara, who was very bad tempered and who always caused other people to get angry. When asked why he kept him, Atisha explained that he did so in order to practice patience, for without patience you could not become a great yogi. It is very useful to think like this.

Even if the sentient being who is giving us trouble is not the Buddha, by treating them as if they are, we can only benefit. It is part of the thought-transformation teachings that we see all sentient beings as equal to the buddhas, not in their realizations, of course, but just as the buddhas are instrumental in our enlightenment by guiding us, so too are sentient beings in helping us develop the qualities we need.

Without the angry person, we can never develop patience; without the needy person, we can never develop generosity and compassion, and so on.

We can view any situation from many perspectives. Rather than seeing somebody who is giving us harm as the cause of our suffering, we can see them as the means for our transformation, as the embodiment of our guru, thinking that our guru has manifested in this way in order for us to develop our patience. As enlightenment is impossible without the perfection of patience, it is impossible without this person trying to harm us and thereby testing our patience. Thinking like that, we see there is no reason to become angry in return. Techniques like this make the mind malleable and able to transform more quickly. This is another benefit of patience.

When somebody criticizes us, pointing out our mistakes to us, it might be natural to get upset, but we should understand how, by destroying our pride, that person is actually doing us a great favor. Pride and arrogance are great faults; they block our spiritual progress. It is said in the teachings that having pride is the cause to be reborn in the future as a slave or as blind, ugly, and repulsive, and with very little capacity to do things. We are not only unable to help others but unable to help ourselves as well.

A person whose mind is filled with pride is like a ball, and any good qualities are like water put on top of the ball—it slides off, unable to stay on top. If we are proud or arrogant, we refuse to learn from others; thinking we know best is a great hindrance to developing on the path and attaining realizations. And so, when somebody deflates our pride, making us become humble, they are teaching us a great lesson.

We can also use poverty in a positive way. Although nobody chooses to be poor, there are many benefits when we find we are. Poverty not only destroys our pride and arrogance but also helps us develop our compassion; we see there are countless others suffering from poverty in just the same way as we are, and compassion naturally arises. Empathy naturally arises for somebody suffering in a similar way. For example, somebody with cancer might initially have so much fear, but having the cancer also allows them to see how terrified others with cancer must feel. Seeing this, they feel great compassion and the wish to help arises.

Only Our Enemy Allows Us to Practice Patience

102 "But my enemy hinders my good works—"
      this is no reason for anger.
      There is no austerity like patience—
      are they not giving me the opportunity to practice it?

103 If I am not patient with my enemy,
      the fault is mine:
      it is I who hinder my own virtue,
      while he remains the potential cause of my virtue.

104 If the one cannot exist without the other,
      if when one is present the other is possible,
      then the first is the cause of the second.
      Why would I call it a hindrance then?

We can develop our patience only with somebody who tries to harm us in some way. The Buddha has given us incredible teachings on patience, but we can't practice patience with the Buddha.

No other being can stop us from gaining merit, only our negative mind. On the other hand, somebody who tries to harm us is giving us the opportunity to gain great merit by practicing patience. If we don't practice patience when we have a wonderful opportunity like this—when faced with somebody wishing us harm—when can we? And without patience, as we have seen, bodhichitta and enlightenment are impossible.

We are alive today, we survive from day to day, to help others and to work diligently toward full enlightenment in order to be of the greatest benefit to all beings. Our main goal is enlightenment, and here is the being who can directly help us achieve it. Without them, it is impossible. Therefore, rather than harming us, they are incredibly kind.

Even the mosquito disturbing our sleep is giving us a lesson in patience. We are trying to sleep and we hear that *bzzz bzzz bzzz* above our head. We know we are in for a bad time. The mosquito lands on our arm and we know there can be no sleep until we get rid of that little bug. She just wants a little drop of blood to survive and feed her children, but we don't see it that way. Even just hearing the noise, we want her dead; seeing her shape as she lands, we want to kill her immediately.

Because we are trying to attain bodhichitta, we must try to develop the loving, compassionate mind for *all* beings—not all beings *except* this mosquito. We cannot determine that we will never give up on any sentient being at all … but we will give up on this one sentient being, this one mosquito. Is there any way we can attain bodhichitta when we exclude one sentient being? No, it is impossible.

When we include her, however, enlightenment is possible. Due to this one little sentient being sitting on our arm at this moment, we can actualize the five Mahayana paths and the ten bodhisattva bhumis and even the entire two stages of the Vajrayana[46] and attain full enlightenment. Furthermore, as we are responsible for leading all sentient beings into liberation and enlightenment, and as our enlightenment is impossible without this mosquito, she is also the cause of the happiness of all sentient beings: all the hell beings, hungry ghosts, animals, human beings, demigods, gods, and intermediate-state beings.

When we reflect on the sufferings of the lower realm beings, such as the unbearable thirst and hunger of the hungry ghosts that lasts for thousands of years or the unimaginable pain that the hell beings must endure for eons, how incredible it is that all that can end based on the kindness of this mosquito. How unbelievably kind this little bug is! Even the Buddha couldn't finish explaining the incredible kindness of this mosquito.

To give our body in charity numberless times to this mosquito would be nothing compared to the kindness she has shown us. How much blood we have drunk from the body of this being that is now a mosquito in *our* manifestations as a mosquito would fill the infinite space; there would be no space left at all. If all the bones of this being that is now a mosquito that we had chewed since beginningless time were collected and piled up, they would fill the entire space; if all the meat of this being that we had eaten since beginningless time were piled up, it would fill the entire space; if all the skin of this being that is now a mosquito that we had used as clothing were piled up, it would fill the entire space.

Now this being is a mosquito, and in order to live, it must harm others by taking blood from them. Now it is our turn! We led that mosquito to create that negative karma. If we had not harmed her in some way in the past, she wouldn't have created that negative karma and so now be faced with this suffering and with the need to harm us. When she bites us, we are merely experiencing the result of our previous negative action. If we hadn't created the cause, there is no way we could experience the result.

Therefore how dare we kill this kind mother sentient being who has been so extremely kind to us in causing us all the happiness in the three times? How dare we kill this precious object where all the buddhas and bodhisattvas came from?

Before, seeing she was just about to bite us, we might have become irritated and wanted to kill her. But now, remembering her kindness, we feel so happy. We rejoice so much because on our arm we see a precious, holy object, a being of infinite kindness, and a little blood is a tiny offering to make to her. We don't feel any pain as she bites us—just joy, even bliss, that we are making charity like this. Instead of feeling disgust and seeing her as an ugly, harmful creature, we see her beauty, as our kind mother. Instead of seeing her as an object of harm, we see how all our happiness depends on her.

This is just an example using one sentient being, a mosquito. There are infinite sentient beings who are equally kind, who allow us to attain great compassion, bodhichitta, and then enlightenment; who have been the source of all the realizations of all the buddhas of the past, present, and future. Whenever some being harms us in some way, we can meditate on that being's kindness in the same way we have on the mosquito's.

THE ENEMY IS LIKE THE MOST VALUABLE TREASURE

Encountering an Enemy Is Like Finding a Rare Treasure

105 The mendicant who appears at the proper time
is not a hindrance to the exercise of generosity.
When one meets a world-renouncer ones does not say
that he is a hindrance to renunciation.

106 It is easy to find mendicants in the world,
difficult to find offenders;
for no one will do me wrong
if I have done no wrong myself.

107 It is therefore as if a treasure
appeared miraculously in my home.
My enemy should be loved,
for he is a friend in the path to awakening.

108 With our joint effort, he offending, I forgiving,
I will obtain the fruit of patience.
I will first give of this fruit to him,
for he is the source of my patience.

What we get from this person being angry with us is inconceivable; they are offering us limitless skies of merit. Surely because of that they are the most precious, kindest person in our life. Think of how precious we think a billion dollars is, how we would love to have that much money. But even if we did, it would be nothing compared with what that person has given us with their anger, allowing us the opportunity to practice patience. Even if we were to offer them all our possessions or all the wealth there is on earth, we could not start to repay their kindness.

They are not only helping us but also all other sentient beings. By allowing us to develop patience, they protect all beings from our harm.

Once we have developed patience, we no longer harm any other sentient being but offer them only peace and happiness, all due to this person who is angry with us. This is how incredibly kind and precious this person is.

But because this precious being, our enemy, might not be our enemy for long, we must make use of this priceless opportunity. They won't be angry at us until the day we die; they won't be angry at us until we become enlightened; they won't dislike us through all time. If they did harbor strong enmity for many years, then that would mean they were extremely kind, because we would have many years to practice patience. The less time their anger lasts, the less time we have to develop our patience, and so we must seize this rare opportunity.

Their anger may not even last until tomorrow, so we have only today, and of today there is only this present hour. If we decide to wait until we go to bed to read a Dharma book that explains about patience, that may be too late; they may have already become our friend.

Therefore this minute is the time to practice patience, while we have found this precious treasure, this extremely kind sentient being who harbors angry thoughts about us. To fail to do so would be an unbelievable loss. Say we work in a job that pays a thousand dollars an hour. As soon as we arise in the morning, getting to work would be all we would think about. But one day, because we feel too lazy to get up, we miss out on a whole day's pay. That would be unthinkable. A far greater loss would be having this rare opportunity—the person who hates us—and not taking it.

This doesn't just apply to angry people. If we found our home overrun by insects, it should seem like finding a jewel in our home. Whenever we encounter some being who irritates us in any way, we should feel like we would if we put our hand in the garbage and accidently pulled out a wish-granting jewel, the most valuable jewel of all. We would be delighted if we found a ten-dollar bill in the garbage, let alone a wish-granting jewel, but having found this being full of negativity is a much greater cause for rejoicing.

In *Eight Verses on Mind Training*, Langri Tangpa said,

When I encounter beings of unpleasant character
And those oppressed by intense negative karma and suffering,
As though finding a treasure of precious jewels,
I will train myself to cherish them, for they are so rarely found.[47]

The being of a "unpleasant character" is somebody who is deeply ignorant, overwhelmed with attachment and anger, whose cruel mind is capable of committing not just the ten nonvirtuous actions but also one or more of the five immediate negativities, such as killing a parent or causing a schism in the sangha.[48]

A person of such a negative nature is shunned by everybody else, chased away whenever they try to come close, like somebody covered with horrible sores from leprosy. Nobody wants them anywhere near; maybe they even want them banished from the country for fear they will contaminate everybody else with their wickedness.

When we see somebody overcome with intense negativity like that, what should we do? Rather than being terrified and renouncing them, we should feel great compassion, thinking how they have broken their vows and have been driven to this state by their delusions. If we could understand the state of their mind, tears would surely pour from our eyes.

How can we help such a being? We can first try to talk to them, but if that alone does not benefit them, we can try other ways such as giving food, clothes, material things, and so forth, doing whatever we can to change their negative attitude. We certainly don't do as others do; we don't avoid them totally. We need to accept the depth of their suffering and keep them in our prayers, even if we can't physically do anything for them.

We should also practice *tonglen* for them, thinking to take all their suffering on ourselves and give them all our happiness and merit. Putting ourselves in their place is the best way to destroy our self-cherishing mind and develop the mind that cherishes others. Afterward we can dedicate our body, material possessions, and all our merits, imagining giving them whatever they need—enjoyments, medicine, the best doctors, and so forth—and especially the ability to generate the path to enlightenment. Even if we have yet to attain bodhichitta, with strong compassion this practice is very effective.

Those Wishing to Benefit Us Cannot Teach Us Patience

109　If you argue that the enemy does not deserve your
　　　　consideration
　　　because "he has no intention of increasing my patience,"
　　　then why would you venerate the good Dharma?
　　　After all, it too becomes a cause for perfection without any
　　　　intention of doing so.

110　If you think he should not have your respect,
　　　thinking "my enemy's intention is to harm me,"
　　　how would you otherwise practice forgiveness?
　　　Would you practice forgiveness toward, say, a physician
　　　　whose goal is your own good?

111　Therefore, patience is possible only under this condition:
　　　that the other harbors an evil intention.
　　　Consequently, only he my enemy is a cause of patience,
　　　and, like the good Dharma, deserves my veneration.

There is no doubt that our guru is extremely kind, but unless we take what he or she advises into our heart and follow it, it will be of no benefit to us at all. Similarly, the Dharma itself has incredible potential to be of benefit, allowing us to destroy all our delusions and create infinite merit. If we don't practice it, however, it is of no benefit to us.

It is incorrect to think that the enemy, who is of great benefit to us in developing our patience, is not kind just because they have no intention to help. The holy Dharma itself doesn't have an intention to benefit us. The two truths[49]—conventional truth and ultimate truth—have no such intention, and the teachings on karma have no such intention. But when we study them and apply them in our life, they are of incredible benefit. By taking refuge in the Dharma, we free ourselves from the lower realms and even from the whole of samsara, and ultimately attain enlightenment. Because the enemy, like the Dharma, has the potential to greatly benefit us, we should venerate them as we do the Dharma.

Even though the Buddha and all the gurus have taught us everything we need to know about developing patience, because they have only compassion for us and could never harm us, there is no way we can practice patience with them. We can only do that with a nonenlightened being—a friend, stranger, or enemy—and it must be somebody who opposes us in some way. As Shantideva said, if everybody tried to help us, like our doctor does, how could we practice patience? We can't practice patience with a friend who wishes only happiness for us, or with a stranger who neither helps nor harms us.

The only type of sentient being we can practice patience with is somebody who wishes us harm. Our virtuous teacher might have given us the teachings, but this person is the one who allows us to put those teachings into practice and in that way is also a virtuous teacher.

Seen like that, the enemy is definitely the kindest, most precious being. Having the chance to practice patience is like having medicine in our house in case of emergency. In fact, taking the medicine of patience is far more important than taking medicine for the body.

Our enemy is as precious as the Buddha or our own kind guru; they are as precious as the doctor who prescribes the medicine that can save our life. Just as we feel so grateful to the Buddha, to our guru, and to our doctor, we should similarly feel grateful to our enemy, our teacher of patience.

Khunu Lama Rinpoche told this story of a meditator meditating on patience. In Lhasa, in previous times, there was a wall around the main temples that housed the wonderful statues, such as the Shakyamuni Buddha statue that the wives of King Songtsen Gampo brought from China and Nepal. People made pilgrimages from all over Tibet, traveling hundreds of miles by foot, to circumambulate the temples by doing full-length prostrations outside the wall.

Once, a prostrator circumambulating in this way, seeing a meditator, asked him what he was doing. The meditator replied he was meditating on patience. The prostrator then shouted at him, "Well, if you are meditating on patience, you had better eat kaka!" The meditator immediately lost his temper and shouted back, "*You* eat kaka!" Even though just seconds before he was meditating on patience, just hearing those words made him lose his temper and immediately retaliate.

Rinpoche explained that bodhisattvas are not like this at all. Their only thought is to be of benefit to all sentient beings, and so, even if somebody harms them, that altruistic mind would never wish to retaliate. A bodhisattva will always give help in return for harm.

Without patience, no matter how much education we have, there is no peace or freedom at all. Our mind becomes the servant to our anger, completely under its control. We educate ourselves in order to be happy; we find a well-paid job in order to be happy. And yet without the practice of the good heart, nothing brings us peace and happiness, nothing protects our mind from suffering or from its causes—ignorance and dissatisfaction.

As long as we follow attachment, as long as we are a friend of our self-cherishing, we easily become impatient and angry, and we are easily hurt by somebody who tries to harm us. On the other hand, when we are patient, nothing bothers or harms us.

At present, our mind is rough, troubled, in bad shape, like a twisted piece of wood. The enemy is like a sharp axe or chisel that we can use to shape that wood into a beautiful object. By using their animosity like a tool, we can develop our good heart, our patience, our compassion. We can't learn patience from trees or rocks. We can only learn patience with somebody who tests it. Another analogy is the whetting stone. If the axe is not sharp, we cannot cut down firewood and have the comfort of a good fire. We need to hone the axe on a stone. In that way, the enemy is like the stone, honing our mind, making us kinder, more patient, and more compassionate.

6 ⁝ WHEN WE RESPECT SENTIENT BEINGS, WE RESPECT THE BUDDHAS

VERSES 112–134

SEEING THE EQUALITY OF SENTIENT BEINGS AND BUDDHAS

Sentient Beings and Buddhas Are Equal in Deserving Our Respect

112 This is why the Sage has declared
    that "the field of living beings is one of the fields of merit,
    the victorious conquerors are another field."
    For many have reached the highest goal by serving them.

113 If one can find in both sentient beings and victorious
        conquerors
    an equal access to the virtues of a buddha,
    why is there this distinction of levels that refuses to
        sentient beings
    the same respect shown to the victorious conquerors?

114 The value of the intention is not derived from any intrin-
        sic quality, but from its ultimate effect.
    Therefore, the value of the intention of sentient beings
    is the same as that of the victorious conquerors,
    and they themselves are consequently equal to the
        victorious conquerors.

115 The exalted character of sentient beings is due
    only to the fact that one who has benevolent intentions
        toward them is worthy of veneration.

> The exalted character of buddhas is due
> only to the fact that one derives merit from faith in them.

116   Living beings can be compared to buddhas
> because they can contribute and participate in the attainment
>   of buddhahood,
> but in reality there is not one among them who could
>   be compared
> to the buddhas, who are oceans of unfathomable virtue.

Compassion for all sentient beings with the exception of one—the one we consider our enemy—is not great compassion, and without great compassion bodhichitta and enlightenment are impossible. Great compassion entails not only the wish for all sentient beings to be free from all suffering but also the determination that we ourselves will free them. This great compassion therefore relies on each and every sentient being: every hell being, hungry ghost, animal, human, demigod, god, and intermediate-state being. It includes our friends and those we consider strangers, but it also includes our enemies.

Shantideva compared the "field" of sentient beings to a buddha field. Because farmers rely on their fields of crops to earn their living, they take very good care of them—watering them, fertilizing them, protecting them from frost, and so forth. They think their crops are extremely precious. In exactly the same way, if we use the field of sentient beings to plant the thoughts of loving-kindness, compassion, and bodhichitta, we reap the crop of full enlightenment.

When we understand that all sentient beings are the field from which we receive all happiness, up to and including enlightenment, we will naturally want to take the best possible care of them, serving them in whatever way is best to repay their kindness. Even if we must give up our life—even if we must give up our life numberless times—there is still no way we can repay that kindness.

At present, we respect the Buddha, Dharma, and Sangha and make offerings to them, because it is through relying on their guidance that we can attain enlightenment. When we understand that we equally need to rely on all sentient beings to obtain buddhahood, through practicing the six perfections with them, we will see that we should also respect and make offerings to them in the same way we do with the Three Rare Sublime Ones. Of course, the buddhas' qualities are inexpressible and their intentions for us are unimaginable, and this is certainly not so for sentient beings. But, as Shantideva said, even though they are not equal in their qualities, they are equal in the results we obtain from them, so why do we not equally revere them?

To attain bodhichitta, we need to create an immense amount of merit through practices such as making offerings to holy objects. How could we make such offerings if it weren't for sentient beings? Even a tiny stick of incense or a few grains of rice have come from the work of others. When we fly above a great city at night and see the millions of lights, these are an excellent offering to the buddhas, but who created all those lights? Sentient beings. If there were no sentient beings, there would be nothing to offer the buddhas. And there would be no buddhas, because they became buddhas by relying on the field of sentient beings.

Sentient beings are the foundation of our practice of generosity and morality, the cause of this perfect human rebirth. They are the foundation of our entire happiness, including enlightenment. They are our merit field, allowing us to create infinite merit by serving them. In that way, they are so kind. We cannot point to one sentient being who is kinder than any other. The whole path depends on all sentient beings.

Paying respect to sentient beings is the same as paying respect to the buddhas and bodhisattvas. If we help sentient beings, that is the best offering to the buddhas and bodhisattvas. If we take care of sentient beings, we take care of the buddhas and bodhisattvas.

When we work for sentient beings, we work for the buddhas and bodhisattvas, because that is all that they are ever doing. There is not one flea, one mosquito, one hell being, one god, one spirit that all buddhas and bodhisattvas, with their infinite wisdom and compassion, are not ceaselessly and tirelessly working for. When we save the life of that flea, we are doing the work of a buddha. When we cherish that angry person, we are doing the work of a buddha, because that is what the buddhas and bodhisattvas do. They cherish every being more than themselves. If we are unable to do that yet, by aspiring to and working toward that, we are pleasing all the buddhas and bodhisattvas.

When we understand the incredible kindness of sentient beings, we can develop loving-kindness and compassion for them. We can see that the only thing they want is happiness and to avoid all suffering, but while they are deluded there is no way they can attain even a little temporal happiness. And yet they are the source of all our past, present, and future happiness, including our eventual enlightenment. This is the main point we should feel in our heart.

Regardless of whether a sentient being loves us, we should sincerely wish them happiness from our heart, with a mind like clear water, unhindered by attachment or other emotional minds that cloud it. With such an attitude, no matter what they do to us, that mind of loving-kindness and compassion does not budge. The deep peace we get from them is something we couldn't get from all the wealth in the world.

Sentient Beings Deserve Our Respect Because of Their Buddha Nature

117   If one could find in a living being even a single atom
        of the virtue of one of these unique accumulations of virtue
            called "a buddha,"
        the three world realms would not be enough
        to offer it its proper veneration.

118   But, in living beings is present indeed, and most excellent,
        a fragment of this faculty of producing the nature of
            buddhahood.
        One should offer veneration to living beings
        in proportion to this partial capacity.

Whereas we are correct in revering the buddhas because of their great qualities, these qualities are there in potential in all living beings. The nature of the mind of every sentient being is clear light; this is called our buddha nature. If we did not have this, there would be no way we could become completely enlightened. The mind is defined as that which is clear and able to perceive objects. Unlike the body, which is tangible—with color, shape, and form—the mind is colorless, shapeless, and formless. Only transient obscurations block the mind from perceiving things clearly, as they are. Empty from its own side, the mind has the potential already there. It is just a question of the right conditions coming together to actualize that potential.

We should understand that there is no distinction at all between the ultimate nature of a sentient being's deluded mind and that of a buddha's immaculate mind. In emptiness there is no such thing as "pure" and "impure." Because there is no inherent deluded mind, it is possible to remove all delusions from the mind and to achieve all the realizations and attain omniscience. This is true of every sentient being. Like the sky covered in clouds is not the clouds, or the mirror covered in dust is not the dust, our mind is not our delusions. No matter how strong a being's anger might be, they have the potential to remove even the imprints of anger from their mind, and the same is true with attachment, jealousy, and so forth. The essential quality of the mind is its purity; all obscurations are only temporary.

Cloudy weather happens because of causes and conditions coming together. Similarly, when other conditions happen, such as wind scattering the clouds, the sky becomes clear. When the delusions that temporarily obscure our mind due to causes and conditions are removed due to other causes and conditions, then the mind's purity can manifest.

Just as a gong has the potential to make a sound, but it needs a stick and somebody using the stick to hit it to produce that sound, our buddha potential will be realized only when all the right causes and conditions are actualized. This can only really happen with this precious human body that we now have, something that animals such as crocodiles, cats, fleas, and so forth do not have. We could explain the whole path to our pet cat for an eon and it would still be unable to comprehend one word of it. On the other hand, we can use that knowledge to develop our mind and clear away our obscurations and develop our positive qualities. Within a few seconds of somebody explaining it to us, we can know with certainty that nonvirtuous actions lead to suffering and virtuous actions lead to happiness. That is something our cat cannot know.

Because at the most fundamental level there is no distinction between the mind of a buddha and that of a deluded sentient being, each deserves our equal respect. The difference is, of course, that we sentient beings have delusions and buddhas don't.

At present, we have acquired not just a human body but also a perfect human rebirth where we are able to begin to allow our buddha nature to manifest. Other sentient beings also have this potential, but because the conditions are not there for them, their buddha nature remains dormant. This gives us a unique opportunity that they don't have at present; it also gives us a huge responsibility. For the brief period we are in this human body, we can waste these perfect conditions we now have or we can use them to develop our potential and to help all other beings.

With this precious human body we have unbelievable freedom, limitless as the sky. If I am asked, "What is the meaning of this life? How can we use what we have?" I always reply that it is to help others in whatever way we can. We can give material comfort and safety to animals and humans, giving them food, shelter, and whatever they need physically. And for many humans we can give mental comfort, praising them and making them feel happy. More important than that is helping them to have happiness in all future lives. The most important service we can do for others, however, is to lead them to liberation and full enlightenment, to allow them to realize their full potential and become omniscient. That is the meaning of our perfect human rebirth.

ENLIGHTENMENT COMES ONLY THROUGH SERVING OTHERS

Serving Sentient Beings Pleases the Buddhas

119 How else could we express our gratitude
to our true friends, incomparable benefactors,

the buddhas and bodhisattvas,
if we did not dedicate ourselves to serving living beings?

120 Buddhas and bodhisattvas will tear their bodies,
and descend into the avichi hell for the sake of these
sentient beings.
Whatever I do for the sake of these sentient beings is
well done.
Therefore, I must in every respect behave kindly toward my
worst enemies.

121 How could I feel pride instead of humility
for these masters, for whose sake my Masters
have freely and without regret
given even their lives.

122 When sentient beings are happy, the monarchs among
sages rejoice;
if they suffer, buddhas are distressed.
Buddhas find satisfaction when living beings are satisfied.
The sages are hurt when a sentient being is offended or
harmed.

123 Like someone whose body is totally enveloped in flames
will find no pleasure in any sense object whatsoever,
in the same manner those whose whole being is compassion
will find no reason for joy as long as living beings
are suffering.

Arya Asanga[50] said that benefiting one sentient being is more meaningful than making offerings not just to one buddha but to buddhas
and bodhisattvas equaling the atoms of the world. This is because
helping sentient beings is the very best offering we can make to the
buddhas.

When we have bodhichitta, offering any service to a sentient being is the happiest thing in our life. Even before reaching that stage, we can understand how every happiness we have ever experienced comes from every sentient being and so see how incredibly kind they are. From that, the spontaneous wish to help them arises. Then we offer whatever help we can, wherever it is needed, even the tiniest thing. Seeing how precious sentient beings are, we are so happy to help whenever we have the opportunity.

This is not something that comes naturally. We are habituated to following our own self-interest, unlike the buddhas and bodhisattvas, who utterly disregard their own interests and only work tirelessly for all other sentient beings.

When we consider the kindness of others, it is unthinkable that we ignore them all and thoughtlessly just enjoy ourselves. It would be like sitting up in the bough of a tree heartlessly looking down at our kind mother being attacked by a tiger. We have eyes, we have the eye of wisdom, whereas our kind mother sentient beings are blind and have no opportunity to help themselves. How can we turn our back on them while they are drowning in such great suffering?

We need to turn our attitude around and learn to work only for others. We have a choice to make every second of the day—either we work for our own selfish interests or for others. We are used to making choices, but before, our choices would have been between the better of two samsaric situations or between profit or loss at work. Now the choice is so simple. Do we choose to do something beneficial or something destructive? Do we take the essence of this precious life or waste it? Do we benefit others (and therefore ourselves) or do we follow self-interest and ensure suffering for ourselves and others? In every second we have the freedom to choose between enlightenment or hell, even in the smallest, most insignificant action. Profit or loss—real profit or loss—the choice is completely in our hands.

Choosing to work solely for others is something that pleases all the buddhas and bodhisattvas. Each sentient being is cherished by the buddhas and bodhisattvas like a mother cherishes her only child. Just as a loving mother wishes only what is best for her child, and she is delighted when they are praised and upset when they are criticized, the buddhas and bodhisattvas feel this for all sentient beings. They are pleased when sentient beings receive happiness and displeased when they receive harm. That does not mean they become angry. When they see sentient beings being harmed, they are displeased but they still have great compassion, both for the harmer and the harmed.

We can make extensive offerings to the buddhas and bodhisattvas of the richest things but at the same time be heedless of harming others. We can even sacrifice animals as offerings to them, as happens in some religions. How can that ever please the buddhas and bodhisattvas? As Shantideva said, we please the buddhas and bodhisattvas when we please sentient beings and we displease the buddhas and bodhisattvas when we harm them.

What is the best offering to the buddhas and bodhisattvas? What pleases them the most? Material possessions mean nothing to them. They are pleased when we offer them things because of the merit we create, not because of the offering itself. What most pleases them is when we strive to become a better person, when we practice the Dharma as well as we are able, working toward attaining realizations and attaining enlightenment. Our real offering is being of benefit to sentient beings, helping them free themselves from suffering and attain all the happinesses: temporal happiness, the happiness of future lives, and (of course) liberation and enlightenment, the very best offering we can make. As Shantideva said in chapter 1 of *A Guide to the Bodhisattva's Way of Life*,

> By simply desiring to benefit others one goes beyond the merit
> that can be derived from worshipping the awakened ones;
> how much more will arise then
> from the actual effort to bring all happiness to all living beings?[51]

Just the wish to benefit others creates far more merit than making extensive offerings to all the buddhas and bodhisattvas, so there is no need to mention actually working toward others' welfare. If we hold this attitude throughout the day, then whatever we do will bring us the greatest joy. We will be working for sentient beings twenty-four hours a day no matter what we do, and nothing pleases the buddhas and bodhisattvas more.

Serving Others Is Serving the Buddhas

124 Therefore, since I have caused pain to other human beings,
    I have brought sorrow to all the compassionate ones.
    Therefore, I confess today my wrongdoing.
    May the sages forgive me for having caused them so
        much distress.

125 In order to gratify the tathagatas,[52]
    today I turn my whole being into the slave of the world.
    May the flood of humanity place their feet on my head.
    May they strike me, that the world protectors may
        be satisfied.

126 The compassionate ones have made the whole world their
        own body,
    there is no doubt about this.
    Then, is it not the protectors themselves who appear
    under the guise of living beings? How could I despise them?

127 Only in this way will I serve the tathagatas,
    only in this way will I reach my aim,
    only thus will I quell the suffering of the world;
    therefore, let this be my vow.

With a Mahayana motivation, every action we do leads us to the precious mind of bodhichitta, the mind that wishes to attain enlightenment in order to benefit all sentient beings. This is the mind that leads us away from the damaging, dangerous misconception that we are the most important person and that others are here to serve us. We are here to serve others. Selfishness is misery; happiness begins when we start cherishing others.

Self-cherishing is the selfish mind that separates us from everybody else and pits us against them. It destroys any compassion we might have, and, of course, it blocks any chance of developing bodhichitta. Any person we meet is judged by our self-cherishing. If they are richer, more powerful, or better educated than we are, we are jealous and despise them. If they are poorer, less powerful, or less educated than we are, we are proud and arrogant and we despise them. If they are the same as we are, we feel intensely competitive toward them and we despise them.

This is how we have been leading our life—blindly following attachment, using others for our own ends, mistakenly thinking that this is the way to happiness. How can we possibly attain enlightenment in order to free every sentient being when we ourselves have not gone beyond being trapped in suffering? We can only truly help others and ourselves when we develop strong aversion for the whole of samsara, seeing it like a prison that we need to break out of as soon as we can. We need to see it like a raging fire we are caught in the middle of. Just as being consumed in the flames holds not the slightest appeal for us, we should feel no attraction for whatever samsara has to offer us. We need to feel as if we have woken in the middle of a nest of cobras, where one false move will make them strike. That is the degree of awareness we need when dealing with any situation in samsara. That's how terrifying samsara is.

When we accept that this has been how we have been living our life for so long, we must determine to change our attitude completely. We must train to cherish others more than ourselves. This is what really pleases the buddhas and bodhisattvas.

The buddhas and bodhisattva are all around—they manifest in whatever form benefits sentient beings—but we cannot see them as such because we are clouded by delusions. They can manifest as a king, a judge, a minister, a monk such as His Holiness the Dalai Lama, a butcher, a wine seller, or even a prostitute. They can manifest as a hungry ghost, a hell being, or even an animal.

Therefore we must be so careful. If we could easily see who has great realizations and who does not, we could pick and choose who to show respect to. But the great beings can manifest in any form. If we get angry with somebody who has annoyed us, how do we know we are not getting angry at a bodhisattva manifesting in that form to show us something? Nothing in the external appearance—clothes, voice, attitude—tells us for sure that this is not a highly realized being. Our mind is just too obscured to know such things. How others appear to us is generally a mirror to the state of our own mind. Their positive and negative qualities are no more than a projection of our own qualities.

We simply don't know who is a bodhisattva, but we do know that showing anger to a bodhisattva even for a second is incredibly heavy negative karma, resulting in unbelievable suffering in the lower realms. In that case, by far the wisest thing to do is to presume every sentient being we encounter is a bodhisattva and never show disrespect to anybody. Of course, we should never create negative karma in connection with any other being, realized or not. But we are habituated to seeing some as annoying or harmful, and negative emotions can too easily arise, so this is a skillful way of protecting our mind.

We can't see countless buddhas only because our mind is still clouded with delusions such as pride. When we can destroy those delusions, we will be like Kadampa Geshe Chayulwa,[53] who served his guru, Geshe Chen Ngawa, with complete devotion. One morning, after he had finished cleaning his guru's room and was carrying out all the dirt in the lap of his robes to throw it out, right there on the steps he suddenly saw numberless buddhas, an indication that he had reached the level of the great path of merit called the *concentration of continual Dharma*. That was the result of having purified his negative karma and obscurations through offering service with a pure mind of guru devotion.

At first, as our view becomes purer, our understanding of sentient beings deepens and our natural tendency to partiality and arrogance reduces. Well before we can see even one being as a buddha, there will be no place left for pride. But even at the level we are now, we can understand how we are so deluded that we just don't know who is enlightened and who isn't, and so the person we are currently feeling superior to may well be a buddha.

We can use Geshe Langri Tangpa's *Eight Verses on Mind Training*, the most famous thought-transformation text, as our guide. It says,

> Whenever I interact with others,
> I will view myself as inferior to all;
> And I will train myself
> To hold others superior from the depths of my heart.[54]

Seeing how precious all sentient beings are, we naturally want to benefit them in whatever way we can. As I have said, the best way is to show them the Dharma—to help them overcome their delusions and become enlightened. We do this by practicing the Dharma as well as we can. The great yogi Milarepa said that although he had nothing material to offer his guru, he could offer his attainment and that was the best offering. Controlling our negative emotions, coming to understand our mind through meditation, not harming and learning to help others, this best helps others and it is the best offering we can make to the buddhas and bodhisattvas.

The essence of the bodhichitta attitude—to solely care for others more than we care for ourselves—is a total thought transformation, from seeing others are there for our benefit to becoming a willing servant for all others.

All Happiness Comes from Pleasing Sentient Beings

128 By himself a single member of the royal guard
     can harass a large crowd;
     the crowd will not be able to resist him;
     they will suffer patiently at his hands;

129   because he is not alone,
      his power is that of the king's army.
      In the same way do not despise
      those who offend you because they might seem weak,

130   for they hold the power of both the guardians of hell
      and the compassionate ones.
      Therefore, try to please all sentient beings,
      as a servant a wrathful king.

131   Could an angry king
      ever cause pains
      like those experienced in hell
      by one who brings grief to sentient beings?

132   Could a satisfied king
      grant a favor
      equal to the condition of buddhahood one would enjoy
      by bringing happiness to sentient beings?

133   Leaving aside this future condition of buddhahood,
      made possible by service to sentient beings,
      don't you see that the patient person
      will attain even here,

134   while still in the cycle of transmigration,
      good fortune, fame, security, beauty,
      health, joy, a long life,
      and the splendid bliss of a world conqueror?

When people don't know the Dharma, because they see all problems as
coming from the outside, they blame others. And because they see all
happiness as coming from outside, they try to get happiness through
material possessions. They can't see that attaining happiness is impossible unless the causes have been created in the past.

As Shantideva said, no matter how angry a king or ruler might be, no matter what they do to us, even having us executed, they don't have the power to send us to the lower realms. An atomic bomb can explode, but it cannot send us to the lower realms. A deadly poison can kill us, but it cannot send us to the lower realms. Only our negative, self-cherishing mind can do that.

Similarly, no matter how pleased a king or ruler might be, even though they can offer us their entire kingdom as a reward, they can never offer us enlightenment. That can only happen when we relinquish the self-cherishing mind completely and develop the mind that cherishes others completely and so attain bodhichitta.

That is why self-cherishing is so harmful. It is much more dangerous than the worst dictator, than all the atomic bombs, than the deadliest poison. There are many causes of death, but death is just the separation of our mind from our body. Where we are reborn is entirely up to us.

Dying with a mind that cherishes others ensures a good rebirth, either in a pure land or as a human being with all the conditions to continue our spiritual development. Dying with self-cherishing ensures a miserable rebirth. Therefore, just as we would cast aside a deadly poison if we found it, we must cast aside the self-cherishing mind and replace it with a mind that cherishes only others.

For that reason, we must dedicate our life to helping others. It is said there are two main reasons why we must do this. The first is because sentient beings are suffering so much and we are capable of helping them. The second is that all our happiness comes from them.

For a bodhisattva, all beings are worthy of compassion because all are suffering. Bodhichitta does not discriminate between the rich or the poor, between the wise or the foolish. Of this, Khunu Lama Rinpoche said,

> The precious gem of bodhichitta
> does not discriminate between rich or poor,
> does not differentiate between wise or foolish;
> it benefits equally the high and low.[55]

No matter how wise some beings seem or how stupid others seem, all are the same in wishing to be free from all suffering, and the same in being unable to avoid it because of fundamental ignorance. The bodhisattva sees this and so makes no discrimination, but instead seeks the well-being of all equally, treating each the way a loving mother tends to her only beloved child.

We use this example because there is no other relationship that can compare to that of a mother and her child. If her child is ill, maybe suffering from something such as leprosy or dysentery, something that would repulse others, the mother feels no repulsion, only great love and compassion. She will do whatever is necessary to help her child. Day and night, she constantly thinks only of her child's welfare. The bodhisattva is the same. With bodhichitta, we feel *exactly* like that toward all sentient beings.

Even if all sentient beings were to rise up and attack us with hatred, that would not change how we feel about them. With bodhichitta, we don't have one single enemy because we always have love for all beings, regardless of the external conditions. No matter what they do, our one concern is to bring them happiness, as if they are our only beloved child. This is what pleases the buddhas and bodhisattvas the most.

We are so fortunate that we have the opportunity to develop this most amazing mind. We have met the Mahayana teachings on bodhichitta and we have the time and the wish to study them and to meditate on them. How incredible that is! And how rare that is.

It is worth thinking of how few people, let alone animals and other sentient beings, have this opportunity. When we think about the billions of people on this planet, how many have the chance that we have to develop on the path? We could have been born as a peasant or a migrant worker; we could have been born into a refugee family or in a war zone. There as so many terrible lives we could have had that would mean nothing but poverty, hardship, and misery, where there would be no freedom at all to do anything, where it would be just the most basic survival. The vast majority of beings have no choice; they must kill, steal, lie, or do any of the other nonvirtuous actions just to survive. A beggar has no choice, a soldier has no choice. Even a general in an army must order others to kill, creating terrible negative karma every day.

We have managed to avoid all these types of existence. At this moment, we are living in a situation where we can avoid creating negative karma. But we have been even more fortunate than that. There are comparatively few people able to follow any spiritual path. And of those who do, how many have met the Buddhadharma, and how many of *those* have met the Mahayana? We can see that this is the one route not just to attain total freedom from suffering but to gain full enlightenment.

To do that, the perfection of patience is vital. Then, whenever we practice patience rather than give in to anger, we make incredible profit. We save ourselves from so much suffering because we don't create its cause. And by being patient we accrue so many benefits.

Rather than having an ugly body, we will have a beautiful body. We can see this even in this life. When somebody who might normally be considered beautiful gets angry, their appearance totally changes; their face becomes twisted and ugly. A patient person, on the other hand, even if they are not considered beautiful by others, has a very gentle face, one that pleases others and makes them happy. And in future lives, they will be very beautiful because of their patience.

The angry person, in future lives, will be born in a foul, violent environment and be without helpers, whereas for the patient person it will be the opposite. The environment they will be reborn into will be very beautiful and peaceful, and they will always be surrounded by people wanting to help them.

When we practice patience, we will have all these qualities, and all the conditions needed to develop on the path: a conducive environment, a long life, the respect of others, and many more. The ultimate result of patience is to have the very best beauty, the beauty of a buddha's holy body.

CONCLUSION: THE DETERMINATION TO DEVELOP PATIENCE

....

To DEVELOP our patience, we above all need great determination based on understanding how vital patience is. We do this by constantly reminding ourselves of the benefits of patience and the shortcomings of its opposite, anger. Besides the wonderful verses we have looked at on patience in *A Guide to the Bodhisattva's Way of Life*, these are also explained in the texts such as Pabongka Rinpoche's *Liberation in the Palm of Your Hand* and Lama Tsongkhapa's *Lamrim Chenmo*. We should read them again and again.

Even just thinking briefly on the destructiveness of anger will make us determined to avoid becoming angry. Whatever way we look at it, we will see there is no justification for anger and every reason to do whatever we can to fully develop patience. Then compassion rather than anger will arise toward whoever is harming us.

It might seem that we are an impatient person and there is nothing we can do about it. We might see others who have a lot of patience and feel we can never be like that. But we must understand what Shantideva said: everything becomes easier with acquaintance. By training our mind we can definitely develop patience.

At present the opposite naturally happens. Somebody harms us and we dwell on that harm, allowing our anger to grow, going over their harm again and again. Even if we are lying in bed trying to sleep, we can't relax at all, thinking over what we can do to them, dreaming of ways in which we can cause them to suffer for what they did. In that way, we train our mind in perfecting our anger.

In just the same way, we can train our mind in patience and compassion, thinking over all the reasons that person is so kind, so precious.

Just as a negative mind can arise in our mind due to certain imprints and conditions, a positive mind can arise. Any negative mind can be diminished and eliminated—that is its nature—just as any positive mind can be developed and perfected. We can definitely learn, before anger arises, to meditate on patience, loving-kindness, and compassion, and in this way reduce our habit of becoming angry. Whereas before anger would have flared up, we can now avoid it.

Some people feel that getting angry is often useful, that we need to be furious in order to have the energy to change a bad situation, such as demonstrating against a social injustice. They think that the only way to get things to change is by angry confrontation. I think there is always another way to change things without getting angry. We can do something—but do it with patience, loving-kindness, and compassion.

By developing a good heart and patience, we help fulfill the real purpose of our life. Because we have the responsibility for the happiness of all living beings, we must develop patience. With patience, no living being receives any harm from us at all; instead, they receive peace and happiness.

Therefore it is very important when we get up each morning to make the strong determination to practice patience. If something negative happens, such as being criticized, we must determine not to be overcome with anger. We must not allow ourselves to become slaves to anger. We must train in patience like athletes train for the Olympics. They don't just do a little training occasionally; they put great effort into it every day, diligently, strenuously, making themselves fit for the Olympics. We must do the same.

Until we are very advanced, we know we will be challenged by people trying to harm us and getting angry with us, and so we must prepare ourselves. After a few years we will find that instead of it being very difficult to stop anger arising, it will be very difficult to become angry.

The Kadampa geshe Ben Gungyal[56] was a great Tibetan meditator. When he was training his mind, he had a pile of white stones and a pile of black stones. Every evening before going to bed, he checked how many virtuous and nonvirtuous actions he had done that day, placing one white stone in one pile for every virtuous action and one black stone in the other pile for every nonvirtuous action. At the beginning, there were very few white stones and many black ones, but as he persevered with his meditations, the pile of white ones grew and the pile of black ones diminished. Then there were more white than black.

Generally people like to make plans, planning the next vacation or the next party, making lists of what to do and deciding when to do them. We, too, should make plans for our mind training, planning what to do when we meet a difficult situation where anger or other delusions could arise. We should be ready with the most effective antidotes, such as meditations on loving-kindness and so forth. "If anger arises in this situation, I will try to do this meditation. If pride arises in that situation, I will do that meditation." We should make plans like this.

Whenever we read a suggestion in a Dharma book that we feel would be effective for us on how to combat a negative emotion, we should write it down and plan to use it when the circumstance arises. Reading the Dharma is always good, but we must make use of any Dharma advice we receive, not just leave it as an intellectual idea.

It can happen that we do our best not to get angry but still do, and then we get angry at ourselves for getting angry! I think this is where regret is very useful. Rather than feeling hopeless, thinking we can never change, we can see that we tried and failed this time, and regret having become angry. We can then firmly resolve to try again—and again and again—until we start to control our anger. The stronger our regret, the more determination we will have to change.

If the Olympic athlete still loses after years of strenuous training, rather than feeling miserable about it and giving up, they train even harder in order to be ready for the next Olympic Games. In the same way we should train and not feel despondent if we fail at first. What we are attempting is billions of times more important than winning an Olympic medal.

Patience is a quality, a knowledge, that we can learn. We spend a lot of time and energy learning about other countries' customs and languages. If we can put so much effort into something like that, shouldn't we do even more to develop patience? Because this is the *most* important thing we can learn, we should put great effort into it. Without it we can never find satisfaction, peace, or happiness in our life. Having patience will make our life and the lives of those around us happy and content.

Patience is one of the six perfections and a vital element on our path to enlightenment. When we train in developing our patience, we are truly taking refuge in the Buddha, Dharma, and Sangha. Refuge is not an aspirin we take if we have a headache; it is not some temporary fix for worldly concerns. The methods that the Buddha describes are the complete way out of all our suffering. He has shown us the importance of minds such as patience, loving-kindness, and compassion, and he has given us methods to develop them: meditation; taking vows not to kill, lie, and so forth. Whenever we try our best to not become angry, to not harm others but to help them, we are taking refuge. The moment we rely on the good heart rather than the selfish attitude, we are taking refuge, whether we consciously think of it like that or not.

Within the Mahayana, along with taking refuge, we develop the three principal aspects of the path: renunciation, right view, and bodhichitta. Of these, I would say bodhichitta is the key. Developing the precious mind of bodhichitta makes everything else we need to do on the path so much easier. The mind aspiring to bodhichitta makes the practice of morality and renunciation utterly meaningful and therefore so much easier to achieve. Because of love and compassion, of course there is no thought of harming others. And with a mind undisturbed by selfish thoughts, concentration and right view come far more easily.

Probably we haven't achieved the full realization of bodhichitta yet, but even to have bodhichitta in a wishing form is a truly amazing thing. Even with aspirational bodhichitta we create limitless skies of merit with every action we do. Aspirational bodhichitta takes effort, though, and so we should reenergize our motivation as often as we can. Before we start something, we should start with the motivation of bodhichitta. While we are doing it, we should remind ourselves of bodhichitta. When we finish, we should dedicate what we have done with a bodhichitta dedication. That way everything we do becomes so pure, so powerful.

As I have said, it is more than possible to develop patience for the wrong reasons, but when it is developed as part of the six perfections, always done with a bodhichitta motivation, it can bring only huge benefit. Practicing patience is not just for the person seeking enlightenment; it is not just for the person seeking liberation from samsara or the happiness of future lives. It should be cultivated by everybody, no matter what religion, skin color, profession, or age. It should be cultivated by rich and poor, by parents and children—by everybody. Anybody who wants harmony in their relationships, who wants happiness and friendship, who wants love and contentment, needs patience.

GLOSSARY

....

aggregates (*skandha*). The psychophysical constituents that make up a sentient being: form, feeling, discriminative awareness, compositional factors, and consciousness. Beings of the desire and form realms have all five, whereas beings in the formless realm no longer have the aggregate of form.

Amitabha (*Öpame*). One of the five Dhyani Buddhas, red in color, representing the wisdom of analysis and the fully purified aggregate of discrimination.

anger. A disturbing thought that exaggerates the negative qualities of an object and wishes to harm it; one of the six root delusions.

arhat (*drachompa*). Literally, "foe destroyer." A person who has destroyed his or her inner enemy, the delusions, and attained liberation from cyclic existence.

arya (*phakpa*). Literally, "noble." One who has realized the wisdom of emptiness.

Asanga, Arya. The fourth-century Indian master who received directly from Maitreya Buddha the extensive, or method, lineage of Shakyamuni Buddha's teachings. Said to have founded the Chittamatra school of Buddhist philosophy. He is one of the six great Indian scholars known as the Six Ornaments.

aspirational bodhichitta (*mönsem jangchup sem*). Also called *wishing* or *aspiring bodhichitta*; the spontaneous, uncontrived mind that wishes to attain full enlightenment for the benefit of all sentient beings. *See also* bodhichitta.

Atisha Dipamkara Shrijnana (982–1054). The renowned Indian master who went to Tibet in 1042 to help in the revival of Buddhism and established the Kadam tradition. His text *Lamp for the Path to Enlightenment* was the first lamrim text.

attachment. A disturbing thought that exaggerates the positive qualities of an object and wishes to possess it; one of the six root delusions.

Avalokiteshvara (*Chenrezig*). The buddha of compassion. A male meditational deity embodying the compassion of all the buddhas. The Dalai Lamas are said to be emanations of this deity.

bodhichitta (*jangchup sem*). A principal consciousness that combines the two factors of wishing to free all beings from suffering and wishing to attain enlightenment because of that; the spontaneous altruistic mind of enlightenment can be either aspirational or engaging.

bodhisattva (*jangchup sempa*). One who possesses bodhichitta.

buddha (*sanggye*). A fully enlightened being. One who has totally eliminated (*sang*) all obscurations veiling the mind and has fully developed (*gye*) all good qualities to perfection. *See also* enlightenment.

Buddhadharma. The teachings of the Buddha. *See also* Dharma.

Buxa Duar. A small town in West Bengal in eastern India where most of the Tibetan monks who escaped to India in 1959 were accommodated.

Chen Ngawa Tsultrim Bar, Geshe (1033/38–1103). Kadampa master and one of Dromtönpa's three main disciples, the other two being Geshe Potowa and Phuchungwa Shönu Gyaltsen.

Chenrezig. See Avalokiteshvara.

clear light (*ösel*). Very subtle mind. This subtlest state of mind occurs naturally at death and through successful tantric practice and is used by practitioners to realize emptiness.

compassion (*karuna*; *nyingjé*). The sincere wish that others be free from suffering and its causes. *See also* great compassion.

conventional truth (*samvriti satya*; *kunzop denpa*). As opposed to ultimate truth, which is the understanding of the ultimate nature of reality (emptiness), conventional truth is what is true to the valid conventional consciousness. It is also called *concealer truth* or *all-obscuring truth* because, although true on one level, it obscures the ultimate nature. Conventional and ultimate truth form the important subject in Buddhist philosophy called the two truths. *See also* ultimate truth.

cyclic existence (*samsara*; *khorwa*). The six realms of conditioned existence, three lower—hell (*naraka*), hungry ghost (*preta*) and animal—and three upper—human, demigod (*asura*) and god (*sura*). It is the beginningless, recurring cycle of death and rebirth under the control of karma and delusion and fraught with suffering. It also refers to the contaminated aggregates of a sentient being.

delusion (*klesha*; *nyönmong*). An obscuration covering the essentially pure nature of the mind, causing suffering and dissatisfaction; the main delusion is ignorance, and all the others come from this.

demigod (*asura*; *lhamayin*). A being in the god realms who enjoys greater comfort and pleasure than human beings but who suffers from jealousy and quarreling.

dependent arising. Also called *dependent origination.* The way that the self and phenomena exist conventionally as relative and interdependent. They come into existence in dependence upon causes and conditions; their parts; and most subtly, the mind imputing, or labeling, them.

desire realm. One of the three realms of samsara, comprising the hell beings, hungry ghosts, animals, humans, demigods, and the six lower classes of gods (*suras*); beings in this realm are preoccupied with desire for objects of the six senses.

Dharma (*chö*). The second refuge jewel. Literally, "that which holds or protects (us from suffering)" and hence brings happiness and leads us toward liberation and enlightenment. In Buddhism, absolute Dharma is the realizations attained along the path to liberation and enlightenment, and conventional Dharma is seen as both the teachings of the Buddha and virtuous actions.

Dharmarakshita. A renowned ninth-century Indian master and the main teacher of Lama Atisha. He wrote the lojong classic *Wheel of Sharp Weapons.*

disturbing thoughts. See delusion.

eight freedoms. The eight states from which a perfect human rebirth is free: being born as a hell being, hungry ghost, animal, long-life god, or barbarian, or in a dark age when no buddha has descended;

holding wrong views; and being born with defective mental or physical faculties. *See also* ten richnesses.

eight types of suffering. Also known as the sufferings of humans. The suffering of birth, old age, illness, death, encountering what is unpleasant, separation from what is pleasant, not getting what you want, and the five appropriated aggregates.

eight worldly dharmas. The worldly concerns that generally motivate the actions of ordinary beings: being happy when given gifts and unhappy when not given them; wanting to be happy and not wanting to be unhappy; wanting praise and not wanting criticism; wanting a good reputation and not wanting a bad reputation.

emptiness (*shunyata*; *tongpanyi*). The absence, or lack, of true existence. Ultimately every phenomenon is empty of existing truly, or from its own side, or independently.

enlightenment (*bodhi*; *jangchup*). Full awakening; buddhahood; omniscience. The ultimate goal of a Mahayana Buddhist, attained when all limitations have been removed from the mind and your positive potential has been completely and perfectly realized. It is a state characterized by infinite compassion, wisdom, and skill.

five aggregates. See aggregates.

geshe. Literally, "spiritual friend." The title conferred on those who have completed extensive studies and examinations at Geluk monastic universities. The highest level of geshe is the *lharampa.*

god (*deva*). A being dwelling in a state with much comfort and pleasure in the god realms of the desire, form, or formless realms.

great compassion (*mahakaruna*; *nyingjé chenpo*). The compassion that includes not only the wish for all sentient beings to be free from suffering and its cause but also the heartfelt determination to accomplish this on one's own. *See also* compassion.

hell (*naraka*). The samsaric realm with the greatest suffering. There are said to be eight hot hells, eight cold hells, and four neighboring hells.

heresy (*lokta*). Also called *mistaken wrong views*; one of the five afflicted views that are part of the root afflictions. A deluded intelligence that rejects the existence of something that exists, such as karma, reincarnation, the Three Jewels, and so forth, and ascribes existence to that which is nonexistent. It is also holding incorrect views about the guru.

hungry ghost (preta). The hungry ghost realm is one of the three lower realms of cyclic existence, where the main suffering is hunger and thirst.

ignorance (avidya; marigpa). Literally, "not seeing" that which exists or the way in which things exist. There are basically two kinds: ignorance of karma and ignorance of ultimate truth. The fundamental delusion from which all others spring. The first of the twelve links of dependent origination.

impermanence (mitakpa). The gross and subtle levels of the transience of phenomena. The moment things and events come into existence, their disintegration has already begun.

imprint (pagcha). The seed, or potential, left on the mind by positive or negative actions of body, speech, and mind.

inherent (or intrinsic) existence. What phenomena are empty of; the object of negation or refutation. To ignorance, phenomena appear to exist independently, in and of themselves, to exist inherently.

intermediate state (bardo). The state between death and rebirth.

Kadam. The order of Tibetan Buddhism founded in the eleventh century by Atisha, Dromtönpa, and their followers, the Kadampa geshes; the forerunner of the Geluk school, whose members are sometimes called the New Kadampas. *See also* Atisha; Dromtönpa.

Kadampa geshe. A practitioner of Kadam lineage. Kadampa geshes are renowned for their practice of thought transformation.

kaka. Slang for feces.

karma (lé) Action; the working of cause and effect, whereby positive (virtuous) actions produce happiness and negative (nonvirtuous) actions produce suffering.

Lamrim Chenmo (The Great Treatise on the Stages of the Path to Enlightenment). Lama Tsongkhapa's most important work, a commentary on Atisha's *Lamp for the Path to Enlightenment*, the fundamental lamrim text.

lama (*guru*). A spiritual guide or teacher. One who shows a disciple the path to liberation and enlightenment.

Lama Yeshe. See Yeshe, Lama.

Langri Tangpa (1054–1123). Dorjé Sengé. Author of the famous *Eight Verses on Mind Training*.

liberation (*nirvana* or *moksha*). The state of complete freedom from samsara; the goal of a practitioner seeking his or her own escape from suffering. "Lower nirvana" is used to refer to this state of self-liberation, while "higher nirvana" refers to the supreme attainment of the full enlightenment of buddhahood. Natural nirvana is the fundamentally pure nature of reality, where all things and events are devoid of any inherent, intrinsic, or independent reality.

lojong. See thought transformation.

loving-kindness (*maitri; yiong jampa*). In the context of the seven points of cause and effect, the wish for all beings to have happiness and its causes, with the added dimension of *yiong* (beautiful, affectionate); often translated as "affectionate loving-kindness." Rinpoche suggests this is the "loving-kindness of seeing others in beauty."

lower realms. The three realms of cyclic existence with the most suffering: the hell, hungry ghost, and animal realms.

Mahayana. Literally, "Great Vehicle." It is one of the two general divisions of Buddhism. Mahayana practitioners' motivation for following the Dharma path is principally their intense wish for all mother sentient beings to be liberated from conditioned existence, or samsara, and to attain the full enlightenment of buddhahood. The Mahayana has two divisions, Paramitayana (Sutrayana) and Vajrayana (a.k.a. Tantrayana or Mantrayana).

Maitreya (*Jampa*). After Shakyamuni Buddha, the next (fifth) of the thousand buddhas of this fortunate eon to descend to turn the wheel of Dharma. Presently residing in the pure land of Tushita (Ganden). Recipient of the method lineage of Shakyamuni Buddha's teachings, which, in a mystical transmission, he passed on to Asanga.

mantra (*ngag*). Literally, "mind protection." Mantras are Sanskrit syllables—usually recited in conjunction with the practice of a particular meditational deity—and embody the qualities of the deity with which they are associated.

meditation (*gom*). Familiarization of the mind with a virtuous object. There are two types: *single-pointed* (*jok gom*), also called *stabilizing* or *placement*; and *analytic* or *insight meditation* (*che gom*).

merely labeled. The subtlest meaning of dependent arising; every phenomenon exists relatively, or conventionally, as a mere label, merely imputed by the mind.

merit. Positive imprints left on the mind by virtuous, or Dharma, actions. The principal cause of happiness. The merit of virtue, when coupled with the merit of wisdom, eventually results in rupakaya.

merit field (or *field of accumulation*). The visualized or actual holy beings in relation to whom one accumulates merit by going for refuge, making offerings, and so forth, and to whom one prays or makes requests for special purposes.

method. All aspects of the path to enlightenment other than those related to emptiness, principally associated with the development of loving-kindness, compassion, and bodhichitta.

mind (*chitta*; *sem*). Synonymous with *consciousness* and *sentience*. Defined as that which is "clear and knowing"; a formless entity that has the ability to perceive objects. Mind is divided into six principal consciousnesses (seeing, hearing, etc.) and fifty-one mental factors, which include mental attitudes such as anger, jealousy, love, and so forth.

mind training (*lojong*). *See* thought transformation.

Nagarjuna (150–250). The great second-century Indian philosopher and tantric adept who propounded the Madhyamaka philosophy of emptiness. He is one of the six great Indian scholars known as the Six Ornaments.

nonvirtue. Negative karma; that which results in suffering.

om mani padme hum. The *mani*; the mantra of Chenrezig, the buddha of compassion.

pandit. Scholar; learned person.

perfect human rebirth. The rare human state, qualified by eight freedoms and ten richnesses, which is the ideal condition for practicing the

Dharma and attaining enlightenment. *See also* eight freedoms; ten richnesses.

perfections (*paramita*). *See* six perfections.

pervasive compounding suffering. The most subtle of the three types of suffering, it refers to the nature of the five aggregates, which are contaminated by karma and delusions. *See also* aggregates; three types of suffering.

pipi. Slang for urination.

precepts. See vows.

prostrations. Paying respect to the guru-deity with body, speech, and mind; one of the tantric preliminaries.

protector. A worldly or enlightened being who protects Buddhism and its practitioners.

pure land. A place where there is no suffering. In some but not all pure lands, after taking birth, the practitioner receives teachings directly from the buddha of that pure land, allowing them to actualize the rest of the path and then become enlightened.

realization. A stable, correct understanding of a Dharma subject, such as emptiness, that affects a deep change within the continuum of the person. The effortless experience resulting from study and meditation supported by guru devotion and ripened by purification and merit-building practices.

refuge. The door to the Dharma path. Having taken refuge from the heart, we become an inner being or Buddhist. There are three levels of refuge—Hinayana, Mahayana, and Vajrayana—and two or three causes necessary for taking refuge: fearing the sufferings of samsara in general and lower realms in particular; faith that Buddha, Dharma, and Sangha have the qualities and power to lead us to happiness, liberation, and enlightenment; and (for Mahayana refuge) compassion for all sentient beings.

renunciation. The state of mind of not having the slightest attraction to samsaric pleasures for even a second and having the strong wish for liberation. The first of the three principal aspects of the path to enlightenment. *See also* bodhichitta; emptiness.

rinpoche. Literally, "precious one." Epithet for an incarnate lama, that is, one who has intentionally taken rebirth in a human form to benefit sentient beings on the path to enlightenment.

samsara (khorwa). Cyclic existence; the six realms of conditioned existence, three lower—hell (*naraka*), hungry ghost (*preta*), and animal (*tiryanc*)—and three upper—human (*manushya*), demigod (*asura*), and god (*sura*). The beginningless, recurring cycle of death and rebirth under the control of karma and delusion, fraught with suffering. Also refers to the contaminated aggregates of a sentient being.

sangha (gendun). Spiritual community; the third of the Three Jewels of Refuge. In Tibetan, *gendun* literally means "intending (*dun*) to virtue (*gen*)." Absolute sangha are those who have directly realized emptiness; relative sangha refers to a group of at least four fully ordained monks or nuns.

self-cherishing. The self-centered attitude of considering your own happiness to be more important than that of others; the main obstacle to the realization of bodhichitta.

sentient being. Any unenlightened being; any being whose mind is not completely free from gross and subtle ignorance.

six perfections (paramita). The practices of a bodhisattva. On the basis of bodhichitta, a bodhisattva practices the six perfections: generosity, morality, patience, enthusiastic perseverance, concentration, and wisdom.

six realms. The general way that Buddhism divides the whole of cyclic existence, with three suffering realms (hell, hungry ghost, and animal) and three fortunate realms (human, demigod, and god). *See also* cyclic existence.

six types of suffering. Nothing is definite in samsara, nothing gives satisfaction in samsara, we have to leave this samsaric body again and again, we have to take rebirth again and again, we forever travel between high and low in samsara, and we must experience pain and death alone.

spirits. Beings not usually visible to ordinary people; can belong to the hungry ghost or god realms; can be beneficent as well as harmful.

stupa. Buddhist reliquary objects ranging in size from huge to a few inches in height and representing the enlightened mind.

suffering of change. What is normally regarded as pleasure, which because of its transitory nature sooner or later turns into suffering. *See also* the three types of suffering.

suffering of suffering. Also called the *suffering of pain*, the commonly recognized suffering experiences of pain, discomfort, and unhappiness. *See also* the three types of suffering.

sutra. A discourse of the Buddha recognized as a canonical text.

taking and giving (*tonglen*). The meditation practice of generating bodhichitta by taking on the suffering of others and giving them our happiness.

tantra. The secret teachings of the Buddha; a scriptural text and the teachings and practices it contains. Also called *Vajrayana* or *Mantrayana*.

ten nonvirtuous actions. General actions to be avoided so as not to create negative karma. Three of body (killing, stealing, and sexual misconduct); four of speech (lying, speaking harshly, slandering, and gossiping); and three of mind (covetousness, ill will, and wrong views).

ten richnesses. Along with the eight freedoms, the defining features of the perfect human rebirth: being born as a human being, in a Dharma country, and with perfect mental and physical faculties; not having committed any of the five immediate negativities; having faith in the Buddha's teachings; being born when a buddha has descended, when the teachings have been revealed, when the complete teachings still exist, and when there are still followers of the teachings; and having the necessary conditions to practice the Dharma, such as the kindness of others.

thought transformation (*lojong*). Also known as *mind training* or *mind transformation*. A powerful approach to the development of bodhichitta, in which the mind is trained to use all situations, both happy and unhappy, as a means to destroy self-cherishing and self-grasping.

Three Jewels (*Triratna*; *Könchok Sum*). Also called the *Triple Gem* or the *Three Rare Sublime Ones*. The objects of Buddhist refuge: the

Buddha, Dharma, and Sangha. Lama Zopa Rinpoche prefers "Three Rare Sublime Ones" as a more direct translation of *Könchok Sum*.

Three Rare Sublime Ones. See Three Jewels.

three types of patience. Disregarding the harm done by others, voluntarily bearing suffering, and definitely thinking about the Dharma

three types of suffering. The suffering of suffering, the suffering of change, and pervasive compounding suffering.

tonglen. See taking and giving.

Tushita (Ganden). The Joyous Land. The pure land of the thousand buddhas of this eon, where the future buddha, Maitreya, and Lama Tsongkhapa reside.

twenty-four types of patience. Practicing patience related to the eight worldly dharmas within three spheres of ourselves, those we love, and our enemies. This means having patience with not obtaining the four desirable objects of happiness, possessions, fame, and praise; and the same with our friends and loved ones; having patience with facing the four undesirable objects of unhappiness, lack of possessions, bad reputation, and blame; and the same with our friends and loved ones; and having patience of rejoicing when our enemy obtains the four desirable objects and not rejoicing when they face the four undesirable ones.

two truths (denpa nyi). The two ways of relating to phenomena, as conventional or all-obscuring truth (*samvritisatya*; *kunzop denpa*), which is the truth to a worldly mind; and ultimate truth (*paramarthasatya*; *döndam denpa*), which is the truth to a mind engaged in ultimate analysis.

ultimate truth (paramarthasatya; döndam denpa). One of the two truths, the other being conventional truth. It is the understanding of the ultimate nature of things and events, emptiness.

Vajrayana. Another name for tantra; the Adamantine Vehicle; the second of the two Mahayana paths. It is also called *Tantrayana* or *Mantrayana*. This is the quickest vehicle of Buddhism, as it allows certain practitioners to attain enlightenment within a single lifetime.

virtue. Positive karma; that which results in happiness.

vows. Precepts taken on the basis of refuge at all levels of Buddhist practice. *Pratimoksha* precepts (vows of individual liberation) are the main vows in the Hinayana tradition and are taken by monks, nuns, and laypeople; they are the basis of all other vows. Bodhisattva and tantric precepts are the main vows in the Mahayana tradition.

wisdom. Different levels of insight into the nature of reality. There are, for example, the three wisdoms of hearing, contemplation, and meditation. Ultimately, there is the wisdom realizing emptiness, which frees beings from cyclic existence and eventually brings them to enlightenment. The complete and perfect accumulation of wisdom results in the wisdom body of a buddha.

wish-granting jewel. Also called *wish-fulfilling jewel.* A jewel that brings its possessor everything they desire.

wrong view. Any mistaken or deluded understanding, as opposed to deluded minds such as the three poisons, that leads to suffering. In Buddhism there are various ways of defining wrong views. The most common one is the last of the ten nonvirtues, also known as heresy (*lokta*), but it can also be either all five of the afflicted views among the unwholesome mental factors—the view of the transitory aggregates, extreme views, views of superiority of belief, the views of superiority of morality and discipline, and mistaken or wrong views—or the last one alone.

Yeshe, Lama (1935–1984). Born and educated in Tibet, he fled to India, where he met his chief disciple, Lama Zopa Rinpoche. They began teaching Westerners at Kopan Monastery in 1969 and founded the Foundation for the Preservation of the Mahayana Tradition (FPMT) in 1975.

yogi. A highly realized male meditator.

NOTES

···

1. Rinpoche tends to use the Sanskrit term *paramita* (gone beyond) rather than *perfection* (which he saves for samsaric perfections). But because this subject is generally known as the six perfections, we have used that term throughout. "Transcendental perfection" is another translation, closer to the Sanskrit, which consists of two syllables: *param*, or "other side"; and *ita*, or "to go."

2. Over the years, Rinpoche has used many names for this sort of patience, such as the patience of not being disturbed by the harm done by others, having patience for the enemy, the patience of not getting angry, the patience of thinking how dare I hurt the being who harms me, and so forth. Other sources use names such as the patience of remaining calm in the face of your attackers (Pabongka Rinpoche, *Liberation in the Palm of Your Hand*) and the patience of disregarding harm done to you (Tsongkhapa, *Lamrim Chenmo*; and Geshe Lhundub Sopa, *Steps on the Path to Enlightenment*).

3. Ringu Tulku's online biography of Shantideva says he was born in South India (some sources cite Saurastra in Gujurat) to King Kalyanavarnam. He was given the name Shantivarnam. B. Alan Wallace's introduction to Shantideva's *Guide to the Bodhisattva's Way of Life* (1997) says, according to the sixteenth-century scholar Taranatha, like the Buddha, Shantideva was born into a royal family, but on the verge of his coronation Manjushri and Tara appeared to him and urged him not to accept the throne, and so he left the kingdom and retreated into the wilderness, attaining siddhis.

4. Manjushri (Jampalyang), the bodhisattva of wisdom, is the recipient of the wisdom lineage of Shakyamuni Buddha's teachings, which he passed on to Nagarjuna.

5. In another version, Rinpoche says Shantideva married a girl named Tara. When he realized he couldn't live with her, he accepted being thrown in the river in a box, and thus escaped householder life.

6. Nalanda was the great Mahayana Buddhist monastic university founded in the fifth century in North India, not far from Bodhgaya, which served as a major source of the Buddhist teachings that spread to Tibet. His Holiness the Dalai Lama often refers to Tibetan Buddhist philosophy as the "Nalanda tradition."

7. *Condensed Advice: A Compendium of Trainings* (*Shikshasamucchaya*; *Lappa küntü*) is composed of twenty-seven stanzas that deal with, like the *Bodhicharyavatara*, the practice of the bodhisattvas. *The Compendium of Sutras* (*Sutrasamuccaya*; *Dokü le tüpa*) is an extremely short text and no longer extant in any translation. There is a text by Nagarjuna of the same name.

8. In another version, Rinpoche says that he placed his hand on the throne and it got smaller until he could easily get onto it.

9. In present-day Bihar. The capital was Rajagriha (Rajgir), where the Buddha gave the *prajnaparamita* (perfection of wisdom) teachings. Magadha existed from about 500 BCE to around the time of the Gupta empire in the sixth century CE.

10. The three realms of existence where there is great suffering: the hell realm, the hungry ghost realm, and the animal realm.

11. This rare human state, which is the ideal condition for practicing the Dharma and attaining enlightenment, is qualified by eight freedoms and ten richnesses. The eight freedoms are freedom from being born as a hell being, from being born as a hungry ghost, from being born as an animal, from being born as a long-life god, from being born as a barbarian, from being born in a dark age when no buddha has descended, from holding wrong views, and from being born with defective mental or physical faculties. The ten richnesses are being born as a human being, being born in a Dharma country, being born with perfect mental and physical faculties, not having committed any of the five immediate negativities, having faith in the Buddha's teachings, being born when a buddha has descended, being born when the teachings have been revealed, being born when the complete teachings still exist, being born when there are still followers of the teachings, and having the necessary conditions to practice the Dharma, such as the kindness of others. See Rinpoche's *The Perfect Human Rebirth* (Zopa 2013).

12. The three realms are the desire realm (where the human realm is), the form realm, and the formless realm.

13. Pabongka Dechen Nyingpo (1871–1941) was the root guru of His Holiness the Dalai Lama's senior and junior tutors. He also gave the teachings compiled in *Liberation in the Palm of Your Hand*.

14. There are eight hot hells: the hell of being alive again and again (the "lightest" suffering in hell), the black-line hell, the gathered and crushed hell, the hell of crying, the hell of great crying, the hot hell, the extremely hot hell, and the inexhaustible hot hell. For a similar explanation of the length of time endured, see Pabongka, as translated by Richards 1991, 265.

15. Shantideva 1.5.

16. It seems that Gómez's translation has missed a bit and combined two verses into one. In Batchelor's translation (1979), verse 8 ends with "for this enemy has no other function / than that of causing me harm"; and Wallace (1997) reads "for that foe has no function other than to harm me."

17. Rinpoche has taught on these thought-transformation practices in books such as *The Door to Satisfaction* (Zopa 2001) and *Transforming Problems into Happiness* (Zopa 1994).

18. The psychophysical constituents that make up a sentient being: form, feeling, discriminative awareness, compositional factors, and consciousness.

19. Potowa Rinchen Sal (1027–1105) was one of the chief disciples of Dromtönpa and was the custodian of the Kadam authoritative treatises.

20. The *eight types of suffering* are the sufferings of birth, old age, illness, death, encountering what is unpleasant, separation from what is pleasant, not getting what you want, and the five appropriated aggregates. The *six types of suffering* are nothing is definite in samsara, nothing gives satisfaction in samsara, we have to leave this

samsaric body again and again, we have to take rebirth again and again, we forever travel between higher and lower in samsara, and we experience pain and death alone.

21. Lama Je Tsongkhapa, Losang Dragpa (1357–1417), was the founder of the Geluk tradition of Tibetan Buddhism and revitalizer of many sutra and tantra lineages and the monastic tradition in Tibet.

22. Rinpoche calls them Uma Devi and Mahadevi but seems to be referring to Parvati and Shiva. Shantideva mentions Durga, the warrior form of Parvati.

23. Compare with Batchelor's 1979 translation: "The victorious warriors are those / who, having disregarded all suffering, / vanquish the foes of hatred and so forth; / (common warriors) slay only corpses."

24. Shantideva 5.13–14.

25. Of the ten nonvirtuous actions, there are three of body (killing, stealing, and sexual misconduct); four of speech (lying, speaking harshly, slandering, and gossiping); and three of mind (covetousness, ill will, and wrong views).

26. An imprint (bakchak) is the seed, or potential, left on the mind by positive or negative actions of body, speech, and mind.

27. This is the third of five paths a practitioner progresses through to attain enlightenment. The five paths are the paths of merit, preparation, seeing, meditation, and no more learning.

28. Disturbing-thought obscurations (kleshavarana, nyöndrib) are the less subtle of the two types of obscurations, the ones that block liberation. The second type, obscurations to knowledge (jneyavarana, shedrib), block enlightenment.

29. Rinpoche is referring to the massacre at Columbine High School, where twelve students and a teacher were killed and many injured.

30. Shantideva often uses the device of an objector intervening and being answered.

31. Editor's note: This is a huge sticking point for many Westerners. Many UK Buddhists call this the "Glenn Hoddle moment" referring to the time when the ex–English football team manager publicly talked about karma in such a way as to imply disabled people deserved to be disabled because of something they had done in the past. (That is how it was understood at least.) It caused a public uproar, reduced Hoddle to a laughingstock, and did people's understanding of karma no good at all. We do all have the karma to be crippled, or murdered, or become murderers. Over countless lifetimes we have accrued countless karmas. As His Holiness the Dalai Lama said once, when asked about the karma of those on death row in the US, "We're all on death row." The point here is not to apportion blame but to accept that what happens to us is the result of some action we have done in the past.

32. *The Wheel of Sharp Weapons* can be found in Jinpa 2006, 133–53.

33. Chen Ngawa Tsultrim Bar (1033/38–1103) was one of Dromtönpa's main disciples. It is said the Kadam lineage of essential instructions stems from him.

34. Jinpa 2008, 585.

35. For these four ways of practicing patience, see Jinpa 2008, 581–84.

36. Shantideva 9.152–53.

37. Shantideva 7.6.

38. Nagarjuna v. 55, as translated by the Padmakara Translation Group 2005, 117.

39. Khunu Lama Tenzin Gyaltsen (1894–1977), also known as Negi Lama and Khunu Rinpoche, was an Indian scholar of Sanskrit and Tibetan and a great master and teacher of the Rimé (nonsectarian) tradition of Tibetan Buddhism. He famously gave teachings to His Holiness the Dalai Lama on Shantideva's *Guide to the Bodhisattva's Way of Life*. He was also a guru of Lama Zopa Rinpoche. His wonderful text *The Jewel Lamp: A Praise of Bodhichitta* is translated into English as *Vast as the Heavens, Deep as the Sea*.

40. Khunu Lama v. 162, as translated by Sparham 1999, 79.

41. Geshe Langri Tangpa (1054–1123) was an important Kadampa geshe, his most famous work being *Eight Verses on Mind Training*. From Jinpa 2006, 275.

42. Shantideva 8.135.

43. Shantideva 8.129–32.

44. Shantideva 8.134.

45. Jinpa 2006, 276.

46. While progressing through the five paths to enlightenment, a practitioner passes through ten levels of concentration called *bhumis*, or grounds. The two stages of highest yoga tantra are the generation stage (*kye rim*) and the completion stage (*dzog rim*).

47. Jinpa 2006, 275.

48. The *five immediate negativities*, or five uninterrupted negative karmas, are actions so heavy they cause us to immediately be reborn in hell after we die. They are killing our mother, father, or an arhat; maliciously drawing blood from a buddha; and causing a schism in the Sangha.

49. The two truths are the two ways we can relate to phenomena. Conventional truth is the truth to a worldly mind. Ultimate truth is the truth to a mind engaged in ultimate analysis, such as the understanding of emptiness.

50. The fourth-century Indian master who received teachings directly from Maitreya Buddha.

51. Shantideva 1.27.

52. *Tathagata* (*dezhin shekpa*), literally, "one who has realized suchness," is an epithet for a buddha.

53. Kadampa Geshe Chayulwa (1075–1138), also known as Zhonnu Ö, was a Kadampa geshe renowned for his impeccable devotion to Geshe Tolungpa and Geshe Chen Ngawa (1038–1103). See Zopa 2009, 109–10.

54. Jinpa 2006, 275.

55. Khunu Lama v. 31 as translated by Sparham 1999, 35.

56. Ben Gungyal (Tsultrim Gyalwa) was an eleventh-century student of Kadam master Gönpawa (1016–1082) who was beloved for his colorful life, having been a robber before he encountered the Dharma.

BIBLIOGRAPHY

Asanga, and Maitreya. 2005. *The Adornment of the Mahayana Sutras* (*Mahayanasutralankara*; *Mdo sde rgyan*). Published as *Universal Vehicle Discourse Literature*. Translated by Lozang Jamspal, Robert Thurman, and American Institute of Buddhist Studies. New York: American Institute of Buddhist Studies.

Atisha. 1997. *Lamp for the Path to Enlightenment* (*Bodhipathapradipa*; *Byang chub lam gyi sgron ma*). Published as *Atisha's Lamp for the Path to Enlightenment*. Commentary by Geshe Sonam Rinchen. Translated and edited by Ruth Sonam. Ithaca, NY: Snow Lion Publications.

Jinpa, Thupten, trans. 2006. *Mind Training: The Great Collection* (*Theg pa chen po blo sbyong brgya rtsa*). Boston: Wisdom Publications.

———, trans. 2008. *The Book of Kadam: The Core Texts*. Boston: Wisdom Publications.

Khunu Lama Tenzin Gyaltsen. 1999. *The Jewel Lamp: A Praise of Bodhichitta* (*Byang chub sems kyi bstod pa rin chen sgron ma*). Published as *Vast as the Heavens, Deep as the Sea*. Translated by Gareth Sparham. Boston: Wisdom Publications.

Nagarjuna. 1995. 2005. *Friendly Letter* (*Suhrillekha*; *Bshes pa'i spring yig*). With a commentary by Kangyur Rinpoche. Translated by Padmakara Translation Group. Ithaca, NY: Snow Lion Publications. Also published as *Nagarjuna's Letter*. 1979. Translated by Geshe Lobsang Tharchin and Artemus B. Engle. Dharamsala, India. Library of Tibetan Works and Archives.

Pabongka Rinpoche. 1991. *Liberation in the Palm of Your Hand* (*Rnam grol lag bcangs*). Translated by Michael Richards. Boston: Wisdom Publications. Also published in three parts as *Liberation in Our Hands: Part One—The Preliminaries*, 1990; *Liberation in Our*

Hands: Guide to the Bodhisattva's Way of Life; Part Two—The Fun-damentals, 1994; *Liberation in Our Hands; Part Three—The Ultimate Goals*, 2001. Translated by Geshe Lobsang Tharchin and Artemus B. Engle. Howell, NJ: Mahayana Sutra and Tantra Press.

Shantideva. Forthcoming. *A Guide to the Bodhisattva's Way of Life* (*Bodhisattvacaryavatara*; *Byang chub sems dpa'i spyod pa la 'jug pa*). Translated by Luis O. Gómez. Boston: Wisdom Publications. Also translated by Stephen Batchelor, 1979–2011. Dharamsala, India: Library of Tibetan Works and Archives. Also translated by B. Alan Wallace and Vesna A. Wallace, 1997. Ithaca, NY: Snow Lion Publi-cations. Also published as *The Way of the Bodhisattva*. 2006. Trans-lated by Padmakara Translation Group. Ithaca, NY: Shambhala Publications.

———. *Compendium of Trainings.* (*Sikṣasamuccaya*; *Bslab pa kun las btus pa*). Published as *Sikṣa-Samuccaya: A Compendium of Buddhist Doctrine.* 1971. Translated by Cecil Bendall and W. H. D. Rouse. Delhi: Motilal Banarsidass.

Sopa, Geshe Lhundub. 2004, 2005, 2008, 2016, 2017. Steps on the Path to Enlightenment: A Commentary on Tsongkhapa's Lamrim Chenmo. In five volumes: Vol. 1: *The Foundation Practices*, with David Pratt, 2004; Vol. 2: *Karma*, with David Pratt, 2005; Vol. 3: *The Way of the Bodhisattva*, with Beth Newman, 2008; Vol. 4, *Sha-matha*, with James Blumenthal, 2016; Vol. 5: *Insight*, with Dechen Rochard, 2017. Boston: Wisdom Publications.

Tangpa, Langri. 2000. *Eight Verses on Mind Training* (*Blo sbyong tshigs rkang brgyad ma*). Published as *Transforming the Mind: Eight Verses on Generating Compassion and Transforming Your Life*. By His Holi-ness the Dalai Lama. New York: Thorsons. Also included in *Mind Training: The Great Collection*. 2006. Translated by Thupten Jinpa. Boston: Wisdom Publications.

Tsongkhapa, Jé. 2000, 2002, 2004. *The Great Treatise on the Path to Enlightenment* (*Byang chub lam rim che ba*). 3 vols. Translated by the Lamrim Chenmo Translation Committee. Ithaca, NY: Snow Lion Publications.

Zopa, Lama Thubten. 1994. *Transforming Problems into Happiness*. Boston: Wisdom Publications.

———. 2001. *The Door to Satisfaction*. Boston: Wisdom Publications.

———. 2009. *The Heart of the Path*. Boston: Lama Yeshe Wisdom Archive.

———. 2013. *The Perfect Human Rebirth*. Boston: Lama Yeshe Wisdom Archive.

INDEX

ABOUT THE AUTHOR

LAMA ZOPA RINPOCHE is one of the most internationally renowned masters of Tibetan Buddhism, working and teaching ceaselessly on almost every continent.

He is the spiritual director and cofounder of the Foundation for the Preservation of the Mahayana Tradition (FPMT), an international network of Buddhist projects, including monasteries in six countries and meditation centers in over thirty; health and nutrition clinics, and clinics specializing in the treatment of leprosy and polio; as well as hospices, schools, publishing activities, and prison outreach projects worldwide.

Lama Zopa Rinpoche is the author of numerous books, including *The Six Perfections*, *Bodhichitta*, *The Four Noble Truths*, *Transforming Problems into Happiness*, *How to Enjoy Death*, *Ultimate Healing*, *The Door to Satisfaction*, *How to Be Happy*, *Wholesome Fear*, *Wisdom Energy*, and *Dear Lama Zopa*, all from Wisdom Publications.

ABOUT THE EDITOR

GORDON MCDOUGALL was director of Cham Tse Ling, the FPMT's Hong Kong center, for two years in the 1980s and worked for Jamyang Buddhist Centre in London from 2000 to 2007. He helped develop the Foundation of Buddhist Thought study program and administered it for seven years. Since 2008 he has been editing Lama Zopa Rinpoche's teachings for Lama Yeshe Wisdom Archive and Wisdom Publications.

WHAT TO READ NEXT
FROM WISDOM PUBLICATIONS

....

The Power of Mantra
Vital Practices for Transformation
Lama Zopa Rinpoche

Lama Zopa Rinpoche guides us through the most popular mantras in Tibetan Buddhism: Shakyamuni Buddha, Chenrezig, Manjushri, Tara, Medicine Buddha, Vajrasattva, and more. The exquisite, full-color illustrations of the deities that accompany the text make this book a beautiful guide, one suitable for both beginners and experienced practitioners.

Six Perfections
The Practice of the Bodhisattvas
Lama Zopa Rinpoche

"A jewel of a book, containing much practical advice on how we can start working on these six precious practices, even if we are not yet bodhisattvas."
—Sangye Khadro (Kathleen McDonald), author of *How to Meditate*

Bodhichitta
Practice for a Meaningful Life
Lama Zopa Rinpoche

An accessible, inspiring book on one of the most important topics in Tibetan Buddhism, written by one of its renowned masters who has an international following of thousands.

The Four Noble Truths
A Guide to Everyday Life
Lama Zopa Rinpoche

The Buddha's profound teachings on the four noble truths are illuminated by a Tibetan master simply and directly, so that readers gain an immediate and personal understanding of the causes and conditions that give rise to suffering as well as the spiritual life as the path to liberation.

How to Be Happy
Lama Zopa Rinpoche

"Rinpoche works with determination and great sincerity in the service of Buddha's teachings and sentient beings."
—His Holiness the Dalai Lama

Transforming Problems into Happiness
Foreword by His Holiness the Dalai Lama
Lama Zopa Rinpoche

"A masterfully brief statement of Buddhist teachings on the nature of humanity and human suffering. . . . This book should be read as the words of a wise, loving parent."
—*Utne Reader*

How to Face Death without Fear
A Handbook by Lama Zopa Rinpoche

"The reality of death is an important opportunity for spiritual transformation. Kyabje Lama Zopa Rinpoche's combined teachings and practices lead the reader to an understanding of this reality and help the person who is dying to achieve a better future life. Rinpoche's clarity and blessings will be tremendously beneficial."
—Yangsi Rinpoche, president, Maitripa College

Bliss of Inner Fire
Heart Practice of the Six Yogas of Naropa
Lama Thubten Yeshe
Foreword by Lama Zopa Rinpoche

"An impressive contribution to the growing body of Buddhist literature for an English-reading audience."
—*The Midwest Book Review*

Introduction to Tantra
Lama Thubten Yeshe
Edited by Jonathan Landaw
Foreword by Philip Glass

"The best introductory work on Tibetan Buddhist tantra available today."
—Janet Gyatso, Harvard University

Becoming Vajrasattva
The Tantric Path of Purification
Lama Thubten Yeshe
Foreword by Lama Zopa Rinpoche

"Lama Yeshe was capable of translating Tibetan Buddhist thought not only through language, but by his presence, gestures, and way of life."
—Gelek Rimpoche, author of *Good Life, Good Death*

Ultimate Healing
The Power of Compassion
Lama Zopa Rinpoche

"This truly is an awesome book."
—Lillian Too

About Wisdom Publications

Wisdom Publications is the leading publisher of classic and contemporary Buddhist books and practical works on mindfulness. To learn more about us or to explore our other books, please visit our website at wisdomexperience.org or contact us at the address below.

Wisdom Publications
199 Elm Street
Somerville, MA 02144 USA

We are a 501(c)(3) organization, and donations in support of our mission are tax deductible.

Wisdom Publications is affiliated with the Foundation for the Preservation of the Mahayana Tradition (FPMT).